edexcel
advancing learning, changing lives

Edexcel GCSE

Drama

Student Book

D0808633

Mike Gould • Melissa Jones
Consultants: Ginny Spooner • Gillian Emmett • Dave Folkson • Clea Wilcher

A PEARSON COMPANY

Published by Pearson Education Limited, a company incorporated in England and Wales, having its registered office at Edinburgh Gate, Harlow, Essex, CM20 2JE. Registered company number: 872828

Edexcel is a registered trade mark of Edexcel Limited

Text © Pearson Education Limited 2009
The rights of Mike Gould and Melissa Jones to be identified as the authors of this work has been asserted by them in accordance with the Copyright, Designs and Patents Act 1988

First published 2009

10 9 8 7 6 5 4 3

British Library Cataloguing in Publication Data
A catalogue record for this book is available from the British Library

ISBN 978 1 846903 71 7

Typeset by Oxford Designers and Illustrators
Illustrated by Oxford Designers and Illustrators
Picture research by Thelma Gilbert
Printed in Malaysia (CTP-VVP)

Acknowledgements
We would like to thank Brian Ingram and Bobbie Wood for their invaluable help in the development of this course. We would also like to thank the teachers who gave up their time to review the manuscript in its early stages and the pupils whose work appears in these pages.

The author and publisher would like to thank the following individuals and organisations for permission to reproduce copyright material: Quote on page 27 from Phillida Lloyd from National Theatre Education Workpack on 'The Duchess of Malfi' written by Carl Miller; Extract on page 33 from Sacred Earth Dramas: An Anthology of Winning Plays from the International Competition of the Sacred Earth Drama Trust (1993), copyright © David Calcutt; Extracts on page 36 and 38 from Humble Boy (Jones, C., 2001), published by Faber and Faber Ltd; Extract on page 37 from Dinah Wood from National Theatre Education Workpack on 'Romeo and Juliet'; Extract on page 69 from The Pedestrian, Fortnightly Publishing Company (Bradbury, R., 1951), reprinted by permission of Don Congdon Associates, Inc. copyright © 1951 by the Fortnightly Publishing Company, renewed 1979 by Ray Bradbury; Poetry on page 71 from Selected Poems of Takagi Kyozo, Carcanet Press (Kyozo, T., translated by Kirkup, J 1973), copyright © James Kirkup; Quote on page 78 from Oh What a Lovely War (Littlewood, J.), copyright © Rogers, Coleridge & White Limited Literary Agency on behalf of the Estate of Joan Littlewood; Poetry on page 79 "Breakfast" from Collected Poems, 1905-1925, Macmillan (Gibson, W., 1933) Copyright © Wilfrid Gibson 1933; Extract on page 79 adapted from Western Front: British Documents from the First World War are the Private Papers of J D Keddie (88/72/1), held by the Department of Documents in the Imperial War Museum, Every effort has been made to trace copyright holders and the author and the Imperial War Museum would be grateful for any information which might help to trace those whose identities or addresses that are not currently known; Poetry on page 87 "Tiananmen" by Fenton, J., reprinted by permission of United Agents on behalf of Salamander Press; Extract on page 90 from "Survival of a lost rainforest tribe", The Sun, 31 May 2008 (Spanton, T.) copyright NI Syndication 2008; Extract on page 113 from Graham World's Fastest Blind Runner, DBDA (Wheeller, M 2008) www.wheellerplays.co.uk, copyright © Mark Wheeller & Marie Salmon, 2008; Extract on page 170 from Hard to Swallow Cambridge University Press (Wheeller, M 1991) p 27, copyright © Mark Wheeller.

The author and publisher would like to thank the following individuals and organisations for permission to reproduce photographs:
(Key: b-bottom; c-centre; l-left; r-right; t-top)
Alamy Images: Ian Butterfield 56cr, 162tl; David Green 18c; Sally & Richard Greenhill 92r; Itani 18tl; Mode/Richard Gleed 56bl, 56tr, 162l, 162r; David Norton 60, 93; Helene Rogers 56br, 162tr; Thomas Sokolowski 53; Rob Walls 28r; Arenapal: Mark Douet 138; Elliot Franks 132, 173; Pete Jones 15, 34; Marilyn Kingwill 163, 168; Pascal Molliere 120, 123; Shakespeare Birthplace Trust/Malcolm Davies 167; John Timbers 43; Michael Le Poer Trench 29b; Paul Vokes/Crescent Theatre 176; Paul Vokes/Crescent Threatre 157; Colin Willoughby 32l, 108, 154; Suzanne Worthington/RSC 140, 156; Bridgeman Art Library Ltd: Salvador Dali, Gala-Salvador Dali Foundation, Dacs, London 2009 72; Corbis: 18br, 28c; Mary Evans Picture Library: 175; Getty Images: 64, 69, 76t, 91bl, 92l, 125; John Haynes: 28b, 178, 188; iStockphoto: 18bl, 18tr, 28l, 70, 162b; James Steidl James Group Studios: 8-9, 58-59; Kobal Collection Ltd: 62l; Graham Michael Production Photography (c) Graham Michael 2008: 66, 172, 179, 183, 186; Midas Marketing Group / Midas Total Marketing Solutions: 117; PA Photos: 59, 86; Pearson Education Ltd: 10, 12, 14c, 14l, 14r, 16, 22, 25bl, 25br, 25tl, 25tr, 26b, 42, 103, 185, 189l, 189r; Photostage Ltd: 26c, 26t, 32r, 36, 45, 78, 187; Reuters: 90; Rex Features: 29t, 52, 91tl; Royal London Hospital Archives: 62r; Roger Scruton: 65; South American Pictures: 91br, 91tr; TopFoto: 76b, 79, 84
All other images © Pearson Education Limited

The websites used in this book were correct and up to date at the time of publication. It is essential for tutors to preview each website before using it in class so as to ensure that the URL is still accurate, relevant and appropriate. We suggest that tutors bookmark useful websites and consider enabling students to access them through the school/college intranet.

Disclaimer
This Edexcel publication offers high-quality support for the delivery of Edexcel qualifications. Edexcel endorsement does not mean that this material is essential to achieve any Edexcel qualification, nor does it mean that this is the only suitable material available to support any Edexcel qualification. No endorsed material will be used verbatim in setting any Edexcel examination/assessment and any resource lists produced by Edexcel shall include this and other appropriate texts.

Copies of official specifications for all Edexcel qualifications may be found on the Edexcel website - www.edexcel.com

Contents

Welcome to Edexcel GCSE Drama

Welcome to Edexcel GCSE Drama. You will have chosen this course because you enjoy:

◉ expressing yourself in an active and exciting way

◉ working in a group

◉ contributing your own ideas and respecting those of others

◉ exploring ideas by putting yourself in other people's shoes

◉ exploring plays written by other people

◉ creating your own drama work

◉ playing many parts in different creative situations

◉ watching and evaluating other people's performances.

You will have enjoyed your previous experience of drama and want to develop your skills at a higher level.

The ability to work successfully as an individual and part of a group using your practical, creative and critical skills is vital to your drama work. Many of the skills you learn and develop will be highly valued in your future even if you do not continue to study drama. If you do continue with drama, you will have an excellent foundation for GCE Drama and Theatre Studies, GCE Performing Arts, BTEC Performing Arts or a Diploma in Creative and Media.

What will you do in the course?

The **Programme of Study** equips you with essential drama skills to apply to your drama work in each unit through explorative strategies, the use of the drama medium, the application of the drama elements and developing drama from different stimuli.

In **Unit 1: Drama Exploration** you use stimulus material and a range of drama activities to explore a topic theme or issue.

In **Unit 2: Exploring Play Texts** you explore the action, characters, ideas, themes and issues of a published play text through a range of suggested drama activities, and experience live theatre performance as a member of the audience.

In **Unit 3: Drama Performance** you produce a performance for a live audience, choosing to be a performer or to provide performance support.

How will you be assessed?

There are three Assessment Objectives that will be used to assess your work.

Assessment Objective (AO)	Where are you assessed?			Total marks
	Unit 1	Unit 2	Unit 3	
AO1: Recall, select, use and communicate their knowledge and understanding of drama in an effective manner to generate, explore and develop ideas.	20%	15%	-	35%
AO2: Apply practical drama skills to communicate in performance.			40%	40%
AO3: Analyse and evaluate their own work and that of others using appropriate terminology.	10%	15%	-	25%

In **Unit 1: Drama Exploration** you will be assessed through a six-hour practical exploration and a documentary response.

In **Unit 2: Exploring Play Texts** you will be assessed through a six-hour practical exploration and a documentary response to the exploration and to the live theatre performance.

In **Unit 3: Drama Performance** you will be assessed by presenting your work in a performance to an examiner.

How will this book help you?

Edexcel does not set any stimulus material or play texts that you have to study. Your teacher will choose all the material that you work on throughout your course and for your final assessed units.

This book has been designed to support you and offers a wide range of ideas. Your teacher will guide you to work they think will best suit you. You may use complete sections of the book or selected parts but whatever is chosen will help you to learn and develop the knowledge and skills that mean you can have an enjoyable and successful experience in GCSE Drama.

This book will:

◉ provide you with a clear outline of what you can do, how you will be assessed and what is important for achievement in each unit.

◉ help you to develop the practical drama skills you need throughout the Programme of Study and each unit, giving you many practical activities to try out and questions to help you evaluate and develop your work.

◉ support your preparation for your documentary response work both in evaluating your own and other group members' practical work and the performances you see as a member of the audience.

- give you many examples of documentary responses with examiner comments, which you will find at the end of each exploration and at the end of Unit 1 and Unit 2.

- offer plenty of ideas on how to develop your performance skills throughout the course.

- enable you to try out a range of different performance styles in preparation for your final Unit 3 performance.

- provide you with information on the different performance support options.

- offer clear practical guidance, including examiner tips and Examzone.

You will find that using this book with the guidance of your teacher will support you throughout the course and in achieving your best in your final assessments.

Throughout the book you will find the following features:

The strategies, mediums and elements of drama are highlighted in blue so you can clearly see where the **Programme of Study** is built into each unit.

Try it!

Try it! boxes provide practical activities to develop your skills.

Key terms are highlighted and clearly explained in the glossary, to help with appropriate use of drama terminology.

Key terms
- stereotyping

edexcel examiner tip
Examiner tips will help you to improve your practical work and your documentary responses.

Independent research

Independent research boxes help you to contextualise and add depth to your work.

exam**zone**   **Examzone** provides information on how to prepare in the time directly leading up to your final Unit 3 examination.

I hope you enjoy your Edexcel GCSE Drama course and wish you success in the many different drama activities you will be involved in, as well as the final examination.

Ginny Spooner
Edexcel

A Teacher Guide with customisable CD-ROM is available for use alongside the Student Book, including guidance for each unit and examples of documentary responses with examiner comments.

An Exploration and Performance DVD Pack is available for use alongside the Student Book which shows a variety of student drama work and levels for each of the units, with examiner comments.

Programme of Study

What is the Programme of Study?

The Programme of Study consists of the essential skills you need to succeed in the three units of the course. These are the building blocks for all the work you will do.

It is likely that you will often be working on several aspects of the Programme of Study at the same time.

For example, you might use both still image and lighting to mark a significant moment in a piece of drama when exploring plot and action.

The Programme of Study is divided into the four areas shown opposite.

How will this book help you with the Programme of Study?

Over the following pages, the first three areas (explorative strategies, the drama medium and the elements of drama) are dealt with in some detail. For each of the listed features you will:

- find an explanation and definition

- explore ways of understanding and using it

- recognise what's important for success in this area

- try out small activities or longer extended explorations, working both on your own and with others

- make links with other areas, strategies and skills

- evaluate and reflect on what you have done and observed.

In addition, there is a brief overview of the forms of stimuli. More in-depth guidance on these is given in the units themselves.

You can use this section of the book to develop an initial understanding of the different areas of the Programme of Study and then refer back to it as a reminder throughout the course. Programme of Study terms are highlighted in blue throughout this book.

Explorative Strategies

Explorative strategies are ways of using drama to explore topics, themes, issues, play texts and performance.

The strategies you are most likely to use are:
- still image
- thought-tracking
- narrating
- hot-seating
- role-play
- cross-cutting
- forum theatre
- marking the moment.

The Drama Medium

The drama medium refers to the different ways in which dramatic meaning is communicated to an audience.

These include the use of:
- costume
- masks and make-up
- sound and music
- lighting
- space and levels
- set and props
- movement, mime gesture
- voice
- spoken language.

The Elements of Drama

The elements of drama are the different parts of a dramatic performance. These relate to the story being told, the themes being developed and the ways the characters are presented.

The elements of drama include:
- action, plot and content
- forms
- climax and anti-climax
- rhythm pace and tempo
- contrasts
- characterisation
- conventions
- symbols.

Forms of Stimuli

Drama arises from many sources and roots. Many different things stimulate the imagination of those who make drama.

These different stimuli include:
- poetry
- artefacts (e.g. objects, pictures, costumes)
- music
- play scripts
- live theatre performances
- television, film, DVDs, videos
- newspaper and magazine articles
- extracts from literary fiction and non-fiction.

Explorative Strategies
Still image

A still image is formed when a group freezes in a particular pose as if they have been captured in a photograph. This can be achieved in a number of ways; one person might act as a 'sculptor' and 'mould' others or it could be a group activity, each actor deciding on their own pose with feedback from others.

You may also hear still image referred to as a *tableau* or a *freeze frame*.

What makes a good still image?

A successful still image will have an **aesthetic** quality, which means that it will be carefully composed – like a good photograph – and will be interesting to look at because of:

- the use of different levels
- how the characters are positioned in relation to one another
- the amount of tension the image captures.

A good still image will also have a clear purpose. The moment captured by the still image should be important for some reason. It might be the start of something, the end of something or the moment when something changes.

Key terms
- aesthetic

Try it!

On the opposite page are three descriptions of still images for an effective beginning, turning point and end in a drama.

Read each one and then create your own still image for a start, turning point and end. Check your ideas against the bullet points on the opposite page to make sure your still images are as effective as possible.

A start

A body lies slumped on the ground.

One character stands over it holding a knife.

Another looks at the body in horror, a third is frozen in a silent scream.

The drama begins…

A turning point

A character is lying in bed with the covers held up to the chin.

Another is holding the door of a wardrobe open. This character is looking at the character in the bed but pointing into the wardrobe where a third person is standing with a feather boa draped around their neck.

This drama is about to take a new turn!

An end

A character kneels by a suitcase, their thumbs pressing the clasps shut. The character's eyes are closed.

Two other characters, one male, one female, stand watching. The male has his arm around the female; she has her head on his shoulder. Her right arm is extended towards a fourth character who is strapped into an electric chair.

The drama ends.

Evaluating use of still image

- Did your image have a clear purpose, so that you knew what you wanted the audience to focus on?
- Did you compose the image so that the audience members saw what you wanted them to see?
- Did you use different levels and think carefully about how your characters were positioned to create tension in the image?
- Did each member of the group tense their body as much as possible and hold the image long enough for the audience to take it all in?

Links with other strategies

A still image might be used with **thought-tracking**, to find out what characters are thinking or feeling at a particular moment, or **marking the moment** when a turning point in a story is recognised.

Sometimes a sequence of still images can be put together to tell a story, like in a comic strip. **Narration** can be used to help the story flow.

Key terms
• evaluation

edexcel **examiner tip**
Evaluation of your work and that of others is an important part of the course. By discussing drama work and giving and receiving feedback you will be able to assess how well a topic or a play text was explored through the use of strategies, elements and mediums in the Programme of Study, and go on to improve the way in which you communicate meaning.

Thought-tracking

Thought-tracking is stopping individuals during a role-play activity and asking them to reveal their character's thoughts at that particular moment.

Miranda says:
Your tale, sir, would cure deafness.

Prospero says:
Dost thou hear?

Miranda is thinking:
I'm listening to my father's account of how we came to the island but I'm bored. When is he going to get to the interesting bit?

Prospero is thinking:
I wish she would pay attention!

Thought-tracking can help you explore the motivation of your character. Ask yourself:

- What do I feel about the situation I am in and the other characters at this moment?
- Why is my character behaving in this way?

What makes thought-tracking work?

- You think about your character's inner thoughts. Speaking these thoughts aloud helps you – and the other actors – to understand your character and why you behave as you do.

- You can respond to the immediate situation ('I feel angry with…' or 'I'm bored with…') but you can also think ahead ('I'm worried about the visit of my sister who is due to arrive any minute now'). This can help you to think of your character as someone real, who has a life beyond the scene that you are acting.

Try it!

Read the extract opposite. Act out the scene and stop at various points to explain what your character is thinking. Examples have been given for the first two lines.

In this scene, Lee is about to be told whether he has got a place in a school like Fame Academy. Mrs Watson is the school's director.

Try it!

Spoken words	Thought-tracking
Mrs Watson: (*smiles*) Come in Lee – sit down.	How am I going to tell him? He seems a nice lad.
Lee: Thanks.	She's trying to make me feel better by smiling, but I feel awful!
Mrs Watson: Well, Lee, you did a great audition. It was clear you'd put a lot of effort into preparing.	
Lee: Oh, not really. Just did my best.	
Mrs Watson: In fact, there were lots of brilliant auditions.	
Lee: I see.	
Mrs Watson: And yours was very good indeed but I'm afraid it's bad news. You didn't get a place.	
Lee: That's OK, really – I've got some more auditions lined up.	

Paired thought-tracking

Work in groups of four and speak each character's thoughts aloud.
For example:

- Student A says Lee's words
- Student B says Lee's thoughts
- Student C says Mrs Watson's words
- Student D says Mrs Watson's thoughts.

Now A and C should swap with B and D and you should improvise the rest of the scene from this moment onwards, adding new lines and spoken thoughts.

Evaluating use of thought-tracking

- What did thought-tracking help you to understand about each character?
- What ideas about the situation did thought-tracking help you to develop?
- Did other groups have different ideas for what the characters were thinking when speaking the same lines?

Links with other strategies

Thought-tracking could be linked to **still images** or **marking the moment**. For example:

- Everyone freezes in position, except for one character. He or she moves around the other characters commenting on how he or she feels about each one.
- One character freezes, and the others talk about their feelings about him or her.
- The group selects a key moment and creates a still image of it. Then, each character in turn talks about their feelings at this moment.

Narrating

14

Narrating is giving a spoken commentary alongside what is happening on stage.

Sometimes a separate narrator tells the story of a play while others act it out. At other times, a character in the play tells the audience what is happening or has happened in the past.

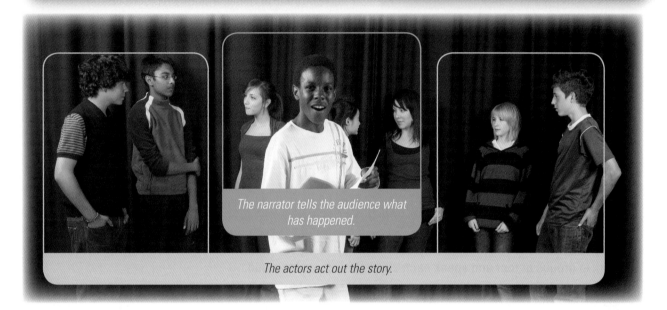

The narrator tells the audience what has happened.

The actors act out the story.

Narrating can be used in many ways. See the examples below.

1. To start a story

> Two households, both alike in dignity
> In fair Verona where we lay our scene…

2. To create an atmosphere or help visualise a scene

> Imagine a city where there are no people, where there are graveyards of cars, where electricity is dead, and dust lies on every building and every street…

3. To bridge or fill gaps in the story

> Many years passed and the forest grew. Everyone forgot that the sun had once shone, until one day when a young woodcutter lost his way…

4. To end a story

> They lived unhappily ever after.

What works well in narrating?

- Narrating should add to what is being seen rather than simply describe it. Narrators generally use different words from the actors to describe events.

- Narrating can be in many forms – formal past-tense speech, song or verse, for example. It can even be used in silent mime.

- A good narrator speaks clearly and projects his or her voice. In traditional drama, narrators were usually separate from the action but modern writers tend to make their narrators personally involved in events.

Try it!

1. Create a mime based on a myth or legend of your choice lasting no more than three to four minutes. One member of your group should narrate the story. He or she should:
   - start the story, and create the mood/atmosphere
   - halfway through, create a bridge between the first part and a later part
   - end the story once the acting is completed.

   The whole group should discuss what the narrator might say and how it is said. For example, think about whether the narration could be in rhyme.

2. Look at the photo below. Think carefully about the image and then make up and present an opening narration which sets the scene, creates a suitable atmosphere and introduces at least one main character.

Evaluating use of narrating

- What form of narration was chosen and why was this appropriate?
- What did the narrating add to the action? How did this help you to understand the events being shown?

Links to other areas of the Programme of Study

The role of a single narrator is often to explain the plot. However, having more than one narrator can be an exciting and different way of making the plot come alive. For example, two narrators could wear different **masks** for a change in the story or mood, or to represent one group of characters against another. You could also try using **unreliable narrators** in your work – speakers who don't tell the truth, change the facts, or interpret things wrongly.

Independent research

Find out about the role of the narrator in *Joseph and his Amazing Technicolor Dream Coat* and *Blood Brothers*. Explore whether they are named characters in the story, and the way in which they narrate. What ideas from this could you use in your own work?

Key terms
- unreliable narrator

Hot-seating

Hot-seating is a technique used to deepen your understanding of a role or character. The most well-known type of hot-seating involves the actor sitting in or on the 'hot-seat' while other members of the group fire questions at him or her. The actor answers in the role of the character.

How do you feel about your brother and what he did?

Tell us about your childhood.

Why did you betray your best friend?

Hot-seating can take many forms. For example:

- The actor in the hot-seat can be questioned by other characters from the play or improvisation. Everyone is in role but it is not an actual scene from the play. The questioners can even be in role as characters who are not in the play, for example, as an imaginary parent or an old friend of the character being questioned.

- Several actors can be hot-seated at once. They can even debate with one another in front of their questioners.

- Hot-seating can be arranged in various ways. For example, the questioners can sit or stand behind the actor(s) in the hot-seat, or they can move around, like police interrogators.

- Hot-seating can go backwards or forwards in time. The actor questioned might answer as a younger or older version of their character in the play.

- Hot-seating can be done as a courtroom scene (e.g. Romeo on trial for the murder of Tybalt), as a police interrogation, as a news report, and so on.

Try it!

With a partner, agree on a story you know well. Decide who will be in role as a character from the story and who will be the questioner. The questioner decides on three questions to ask. At least one should be a 'why' question about motivation. The actor must think of difficult questions they might be asked and how they might respond. Then, run the hot-seating.

Reverse the roles and do the same for a different story or script.

The grid below may be useful for planning your questions.

Can you tell us how you felt when…?	Go over the events leading up to… What really happened?
Why did you…?	Tell us about your childhood…
What made you…?	Why didn't you…?
Tell us about your relationship with…	Why did you say…?

What makes hot-seating successful?

◉ Good hot-seating is often well prepared but it can be spontaneous. Preparing the questions beforehand ensures that the actor in the hot-seat can think carefully about how they respond. Questions that need just a 'yes' or 'no' answer will not help to explore the character in detail.

◉ Hot-seating is successful when the actors and the other people working on a script or devised piece come to really understand the character. It helps to explore both factual information (what they did at a certain time, for example) and motivation (why they acted as they did), and possible new approaches to characters.

Evaluating use of hot-seating

◉ How did hot-seating help you to understand the character better?

◉ Did the hot-seating change any of your views about the character?

◉ What was difficult about being hot-seated?

◉ What was difficult about being the questioner?

Links with other strategies

Hot-seating can be easily combined with **thought-tracking**, **still image** and **marking the moment**. For example, a character being hot-seated may deliberately mislead or hide the truth but a different actor could voice their real thoughts when they are being questioned.

Role-play

In role-play, you pretend to be someone else by putting yourself in a similar position and imagining what the person might say, think and feel.

> What does this person feel, think and say?
> What is their life like?

What makes a successful role-play?

To take on a role successfully, you need:

- knowledge – about the person's lifestyle, background and environment

- **empathy** – understanding what goes on in their head; for example, what they feel, believe, want or dislike. Remember that you do not have to like or sympathise with them (you might have to play the role of a murderer!) but you do need to understand their motivation

- physical awareness – feeling what it's like living in their body; for example, think about how they would speak, move and gesticulate

- a sense of language – consider what they would say and how they would say it.

Key terms
- empathy

Independent research

What do you understand by the word 'stereotype'? Check its meaning in a dictionary. Think about how a stereotypical police officer speaks and looks. What is the danger of using this approach in role-play?

Try it!

The challenge is to take on five roles in 50 seconds! Start walking, and change roles each time your teacher or another pupil calls one out; for example, you might take on the role of police officer, burglar, fashion model, homeless teenager and escaped tiger from the zoo! No speech is allowed.

Try it!

Here are three role-play cards. Working in groups of three, take one of these cards each.

Role A: Young homeless person

Age: 19

On the streets after being thrown out by step-dad after a row.

- Has been on the streets for two days.
- Doesn't know where to go or what to do and is running out of money.
- Definitely not going home.

Role B: Police officer

Age: 35

Has been a constable 'on the beat' for ten years.

- Knows the streets very well.
- Loves job.
- Worries about young people and the problems they can face on the streets.

Role C: Leader of a criminal gang

Age: 35

Controls the begging on the streets.

- Takes a cut from beggars in return for 'protection'.
- Was once homeless, but managed to get off the streets and get a posh flat through criminal activities.
- Knows police officer.

Spend ten minutes jotting down further information about your character – for example, their name, further details about their family, physical details such as height, weight and specific features. Think about their motivation – what does he or she want long term? To go back home, to retire or to go straight?

Perform the role-play in three parts:

- One to two minutes showing your character getting up in the morning, dressing and going out.

- Two to three minutes showing your character phoning someone and leaving a message that is relevant to your role.

- An extended improvisation in which A meets C and then B. Let the improvisation tell a complete story which has a specific ending (for example, the teenager goes home or the police officer is outwitted).

Evaluating use of role-play

- How well were you able to 'get inside' the role you were playing? What made it difficult or easy?

- Was each role a stereotype or was each person able to make their character more complex and believable?

- What else could you have done to help you develop or understand the role (other explorative strategies, real-life observation)?

Links with other strategies

Many other strategies could help with developing role-play but two in particular, **hot-seating** and **thought-tracking**, would help you to put yourself in someone else's shoes.

Cross-cutting

Cross-cutting is creating scenes and then re-ordering the action by 'cutting' forwards and backwards to different times. For example, you could start with a middle scene, then have a flashback to the first scene, and then continue with the final scenes.

Here is a conventional drama sequence:

Scene 1	Scene 2	Scene 3	Scene 4
Marc rows with step-dad, who threatens to hit him. Marc storms out, taking his belongings with him.	Marc on streets, homeless. 'Helped' by gang leader, Vic, and taught how to beg in return for handing over money.	Sheila, police officer, gives Marc advice. Marc rejects it. Vic returns and threatens Marc who hasn't earned any money.	Marc returns home. Step-dad at door apologises and welcomes Marc back.

If you were cross-cutting you might start at Scene 2 and then 'cut' to Scene 1 (back in time). The sequence would look like this:

Scene 2	Scene 1	Scene 3	Scene 4
Marc on streets, homeless. 'Helped' by gang leader, Vic, and taught how to beg in return for handing over money.	Marc rows with step-dad, who threatens to hit him. Marc storms out, taking his belongings with him.	Sheila, police officer, gives Marc advice. Marc rejects it. Vic returns and threatens Marc who hasn't earned any money.	Marc returns home. Step-dad at door apologises and welcomes Marc back.

Cross-cutting can also be used in drama exploration to show more than one perspective on a single moment in time.

What makes successful cross-cutting?

- Ensuring so that the audience's engagement and reactions are highly controlled. For example, you could open at a moment of high drama or climax, so that you immediately get the audience's attention and arouse curiosity. You could also cut quickly between two scenes taking place at the same time to show contrast.

- Varying the pace of the drama to maximum effect.

- Ensuring that the audience does not get confused as to what is happening when – it needs to be clear that the cutting has either moved the action forwards or backwards or that each scene is a different perspective on the same moment. Think about how it would be best to cut between Scene 2 and 1 and then Scene 1 and 3 above. There are some ideas about how to do this on the opposite page.

Techniques in cross-cutting

In films, cross-cutting is a normal part of storytelling, because different images can be shown instantly, for example, flashbacks. This isn't always as easy in drama performance. However, there are some techniques you can use, shown in the table below.

Technique	How it works	Example
Parallel cross-cutting with mime	While you perform your scene, another set of actors shows a different scene at the same time. Your character might appear in both but played by another student.	Marc on the streets, homeless, explains to Vic why he's there. At the same time, a 'parallel' set of actors with another 'Marc' show the earlier scene with him arguing with his step-dad (perhaps in mime).
Cross-cutting with narration and still images	While a scene is being performed, the main character 'steps out' of the action (which freezes) and narrates what has happened to him/her earlier.	Marc on the streets, homeless, begging. The scene freezes as Vic approaches. Marc stands up and explains to the audience why he is there. There is then a cross-cut to Scene 1. You might then return to the first scene, 'unfreezing' the still image.

Try it!

In small groups, create your own drama sequence. Make sure it has some clear stages to it in terms of timescale and separate scenes.

Once you have prepared this short drama, run it in a conventional linear sequence (that is, in the normal time order). Then, explore with your group different ways of re-ordering the scenes or events or of showing a different perspective on the same event. Try to use an inventive way to link the seperate scenes.

Evaluating use of cross-cutting

In discussion, compare and contrast the conventional, linear version with the cross-cut version. Consider these issues:

◉ Which of the two versions did you think worked best? Why?

◉ What different interpretations of events could you draw out by using cross-cutting in different ways?

◉ What worked well in other groups' sequences?

Links with other strategies

Cross-cutting can be used with **narration** and can be combined with the use of **still image** as a way of freezing a moment, while a different scene takes place.

Forum theatre

22

> Forum theatre is a form of drama where a scene is enacted and watched by the rest of the group. At any point in the drama, observers or actors can stop the action to ask for help or to refocus the drama. Observers can step in and add a role or take over an existing role.

An example of forum theatre in action could be a group acting out the following situation.

Two teams of negotiators, during a war, meet to discuss a ceasefire. One side

- wants their prisoners-of-war back; the other side wants the bombing of their

- villages to stop. Neither wants to give too much away.

The performance is watched by others who may already be in roles of their own. During the performance, an actor might stop the action, turn to the observers and say, 'I'm stuck. I've run out of reasons why they should return our prisoners. Help me.'

At this point, an observer could suggest some more reasons, or take the place of the actor and take on his or her role.

Alternatively, at any point in the drama, an observer might go up to an actor, tap them on the shoulder and replace them in the role or take on a new role, bringing fresh ideas to the drama. Sometimes observers are referred to as 'spectators' (a combination of 'spectators' and 'actors') since they both watch and act.

What makes forum theatre powerful and interesting?

- The collaboration between audience and actors to bring fresh ideas to the drama and help each other to develop work.

Try it!

Here is the starting point for a scene that could be developed using forum theatre.

Four members of your group should take on the roles of **A**, **B**, **C** and **D**. The rest of you will start off as observers.

A is a wedding planner. He has arranged to see an engaged couple, **B** and **C**, who are telling him what they want for their posh wedding (where, when, the style and so on).

However, **B** and **C** are very choosy and spoilt and don't like the suggestions that **A** makes.

A is impatient and doesn't like these clients. He is in danger of losing the whole deal unless he can compromise with **B** and **C**.

A has an assistant, **D**, who tries to offer advice, but **A** doesn't listen.

The problem is that **A** is likely to lose his temper, and lose the deal for the wedding. How will **A** cope with **B** and **C**, and will he need the assistance of **D**?

1. Run the improvisation first without interruption for a maximum of three to four minutes.

2. Then continue using the forum theatre approach with observers making suggestions or stepping in to take over a role when they have an idea to take the drama in a new direction.

Evaluating use of forum theatre

- Did anyone make a suggestion or take over a role in a way which you thought was particularly effective? Why was it effective?
- Was there a point at which any of the interruptions significantly changed the course of the drama? Was this an improvement? Why?
- How did the drama end? Was the 'problem' resolved?

Links with other strategies

You need to be comfortable with **role-play** to explore forum theatre. The characters are often not very detailed, as in a full play. Nevertheless you must pretend to be someone else, take on their beliefs, feelings and emotional responses.

Look carefully at **spoken language**. This is often key in forum theatre where the choice of words used is just as important as any actions taken.

24

Marking the moment

After a piece of drama work has been created, you can identify or 'mark' a significant moment in it. This can be done in various ways, for example, through discussion, by freezing a point of action, adding captions, thought-tracking or using lighting to spotlight the moment.

The moment chosen should be important in terms of showing how you understand and respond to the issue or idea being explored.

Marking the moment can be done in many ways. Some methods are explained in the grid below.

Method	Description
Replay	The actors recreate or replay the 'marked moment' so everyone can see it again.
Discussion	Observers and actors discuss the moment. The student who has selected it identifies, with the help of the group, what is significant for his or her character.
Captions (written and spoken)	For example, the moment can be photographed (a still image) and a written caption added in a display or the action can be frozen and the caption spoken aloud. Titles or captions can be suggested or written (e.g. 'Romeo feels real love for the first time').
Inner thoughts spoken aloud	The moment can be frozen or replayed and a specific individual can describe what he or she is feeling at that time, similar to thought-tracking.
Lighting	A spotlight could be used to focus on individuals or groups in the marked moment as they are discussed. Or, a specific moment of dialogue or action could be lit within a scene, as a way of showing its significance.

Marking the moment successfully

When choosing your moment to mark, think carefully about why it is significant:

- Is it a piece of news or an event that has an impact on a character?
- Is it when the character reveals something about him or herself?
- Is it when we see a change in the way a character behaves?
- Is it when there is a change of mood or atmosphere (for example, from light comedy to tragedy)?

Try it!

Look at these four pictures. They are key moments in the story of *Missing Dan Nolan*, a play about a boy who decides to go out fishing with his friends on New Year's Eve and disappears for ever.

When Dan leaves with his friends, his parents remind him that it is important to stick together for safety.

Dan and his friends begin to fish but they also have a bottle of vodka with them and start to get very drunk.

Halfway through the night, Dan leaves his friends drinking and wanders off to buy chocolate.

Dan is never seen again and his parents are left wondering what happened to him on New Year's Eve.

Act out this short drama in a group.

- Select (mark) one moment from the drama.
- Decide why it is significant for you, and what questions remain unanswered.
- Give the marked moment a caption (you can suggest more than one).
- Decide within the marked moment who and what you will spotlight and why.

Evaluating use of marking the moment

- How did you use marking the moment in the work you did?
- How did marking the moment help your understanding of character, theme or situation?

Links with other strategies

Thought-tracking and **still image** can be used in conjunction with marking the moment. For example, once the moment has been marked through creating a still image, the characters, rather than the actors, can say what was significant to them through thought-tracking.

Independent research

Marking the moment is a useful explorative strategy to use with both devised and scripted work.

Think about how you might use it effectively in your work for Unit 3.

The Drama Medium

Costume

> Costume refers to the clothing and accessories worn by characters in dramatic productions.

Costume can:

- add colour and glamour to enhance mood
- help identify individuals and groups of characters. For example, all soldiers might appear in armour and with swords, or a particular child might always carry their favourite toy
- assist with the plot, if the costume changes for a character over the course of the play, e.g. rags to riches
- reflect themes or issues.

Costume design falls into three main categories: period, stylised or minimalist.

Period

The costume reflects the time in which the play was set. So, for Shakespeare's *Julius Caesar* characters would wear the clothing of Rome circa 50 BC.

Costumes from a production of Shakespeare's Julius Caesar

Stylised

The costume is not representative of any particular time in history, but may mix styles together. For example, a Shakespeare hero may have a robe but may also carry a machine-gun or use a mobile phone. Or, the style may have a period look but different from that when the play was originally set. The style may also be based on a theme (e.g. gangsters from the 1920s).

Costumes from a production of Shakespeare's The Taming of the Shrew

Minimalist

The costume is very simple. It may be simple to the extent that we take little or no notice of it (for example, everyone wears jeans and different coloured T-shirts). Alternatively there may be a few simple items which signify character or role: for example, a cap for a sailor, an old coat for a tramp or a crown for a king.

Minimalist costume used in a student production based around the theme of communication

Successful use of costume

The successful use of costume:

- communicates meaning – it is not accidental, but supports the story, characterisation or themes

- links well with other design elements – for example, the lighting, stage design, make-up or props

- allows actors to express themselves freely in movement.

Some theatre directors use costume to ensure that an audience can identify closely with the characters in the play. One theatre director, Phyllida Lloyd, said this about her costume choice for a production of *The Duchess of Malfi* (a Jacobean play):

'It would never have occurred to me to produce the play in Jacobean costume. *The Duchess of Malfi* was a well-known story in 1613, and one known to have taken place in Italy a hundred years before that. Yet, it was performed in the costume of the audience – in modern dress. So we are aiming for the same sense of a shared experience between audience and stage. It's not about connecting it with current affairs or current events, but trying to strip away the things which might stop the audience recognising that these characters are from their own world.'

Try it!

Shakespeare's play *Macbeth* is about a Scottish lord whose wife persuades him to murder the king and take the crown for himself. To protect himself from others, Macbeth murders a close friend, as well as the wife and children of a rival. In the end he is killed in battle.

Shakespeare wrote the play at the end of the 16th century but the real Macbeth lived in the 11th century. However, the play's themes – ambition, power, corruption – are timeless.

What sort of costume would you design for Macbeth? Decide on a style and theme. Will it be period, stylised or minimalist? Will you portray Macbeth as a loyal subject to the king, a politician, or perhaps a gangster? Use a basic figure like the one to the right and draw on a costume design. Label each element to explain your choice.

Evaluation

- Describe your choice of costume and the overall style you were hoping to achieve.

- Explain why you chose this style and whether it has the effect you were looking for.

- What other costume ideas could you use for other characters (for example, the King and Lady Macbeth)?

Independent research

There have been many film and stage versions of *Macbeth*. Do an Internet search for 'Joe Macbeth 1955' and 'McKellen Macbeth 1979'. What different costume designs were used in each? Were either meant to reflect Shakespeare's time or the 11th century?

Masks

A mask is a form of covering for the face. It can cover just a small part of the face or sometimes as much as the whole head.

28

Masks can be used in many ways. These include:

- to create a type of character or to represent a specific emotion (e.g. a devil, or anger)
- as a disguise when a character needs to keep his or her identity secret from another character or the audience
- as a way of representing events in a non-naturalistic way (e.g. during a fight shown as a dance or mime)
- to enable actors to take on lots of different roles and identities
- as part of magical, supernatural or mythical storytelling.

Successful use of masks

This depends on the role that masks play. If they are temporary disguises in a **naturalistic** play, then they need to be fairly discreet and not noticeable by the audience. However, if the mask is designed to tell us who or what something is then it needs to be instantly striking to catch the audience's attention.

Independent research

Many websites deal with the history of particular masks in different societies.

Use the Internet to research the following types of mask:

- Balinese masks
- Masks for Noh Theatre (Japanese)
- Masks for commedia dell'arte.

In what obvious ways are they different? What ideas from this research might you use in your own work? See page 188 for further information on use of masks for Unit 3.

Try it!

Read the following description for a setting and then develop it into a performance using masks.

It is the year 2050. The United Kingdom is made up of two groups of people – those who live above ground, 'The Lightseekers', who are mostly rich and powerful, and those who live in the old railway tunnels, subways and caves underground – 'The Lowrunners'.

Think carefully about:

- the purpose of the masks (e.g. to show groupings or individuals)
- what style would work best (e.g. full-face, half-face).

Sketch out your ideas and annotate them with comments explaining your choices.

Key terms
- naturalistic

Make-up

Make-up is the cosmetic paint, powder and colouring used on stage to make faces and expressions visible to the audience. It can emphasise features that might otherwise be washed out by bright stage lights. In some cases, make-up is used to exaggerate certain features or to create unusual or striking appearances. It is sometimes designed with specific lighting in mind to achieve particular effects.

Successful use of make-up

The success of make-up depends on what it is being used for. If the actors need to look natural, then the make-up should ensure that the audience can clearly see the actors' features but not draw attention to itself.

However, if the make-up is to exaggerate a character, or to place them in a specific historical time, then it needs to be more obvious. For example, in a play set in Ancient Egyptian times actors may want to use heavy eyeliner around their eyes. The make-up on a magical elfin character might need to convey an other-worldly impression by giving a distinctive, non-human colour and shape to the face.

Vivien Parry applying her make-up for her lead role in Mamma Mia

Make-up for a character in Andrew Lloyd-Webber's musical Cats

Try it!

Imagine you are the make-up artist for a play with a magical character in it. Design make-up for the character which reflects where they live or come from, for example, the woodland, sea, desert, underground or river. Draw a sketch and then annotate it, explaining your ideas for the design.

Independent research

Look at the 'How to' guide to make-up in the advice section of the website for *The Stage* (www.thestage.co.uk).

Read the article by Paul Vale. Jot down three or four key bits of advice he offers that you could refer to when applying make-up yourself.

Sound and music

Sound and music are key elements in most drama. This includes everything the audience hears, such as recorded or live music and sound effects, and even the different ways the voices of the actors are amplified (if at all).

In most play scripts there are some references to sound and music.
See below for an example.

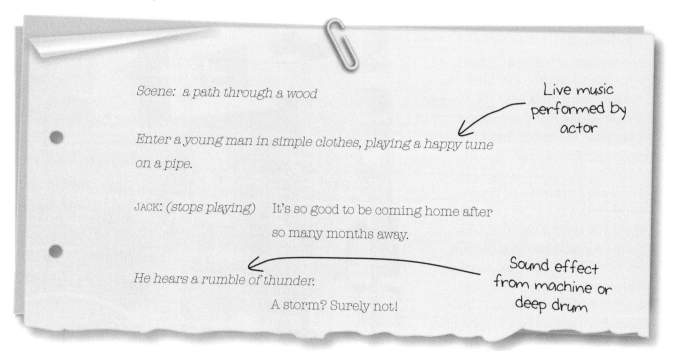

Scene: a path through a wood

Enter a young man in simple clothes, playing a happy tune on a pipe.

Live music performed by actor

JACK: *(stops playing)* It's so good to be coming home after so many months away.

He hears a rumble of thunder.

A storm? Surely not!

Sound effect from machine or deep drum

Successful use of sound and music

Using music successfully:

- creates atmosphere, tone and mood
- helps with the telling of the story and progresses the plot; for example, particular music might be played to convey the passing of time or mark a recurring event
- assists in the way we understand themes, ideas or issues
- helps to shape our view of characters and relationships; for example, powerful orchestral music could be used for a king or queen.

Independent research

Sound effects or music can completely change the mood of a scene. Check this out by playing a couple of minutes of home video or DVD (e.g. of your dog running around, or a family barbecue) without the sound. Then play different pieces of recorded music to go with the video/DVD – perhaps a sad ballad at first, then some upbeat rock or dance music. Note how each one affects how you see the film. There are many examples of animated shorts that tell a story with the help of simple sounds or music on YouTube and other Internet resources. These might give you ideas on how you could use sound effectively in your own work.

Try it!

Read the following script. In groups, decide how music and sound could be added to make the performance spooky. Suggest where you would include sound and music, and what sort. Do the same thing to make the performance comic.

> Scene: a back-street at night
>
> Enter a figure in a dark coat glancing about before edging along the wall towards the corner of the street. As he/she edges along, enter Rachel and Lennie. They stop.
>
> LENNIE: Look! Over there!
>
> RACHEL: Sssshh.
>
> LENNIE: Sorry.
>
> RACHEL: (whispers) Come on.
>
> Rachel sets off. After a moment's hesitation, Lennie follows. The figure turns, and they both flatten themselves against the wall.

Evaluation

Try out a performance with your suggested sound and music.

- How did you create a spooky/comic feel?
- Did the music and sound affect the way people acted? How?
- Did any of the sounds or music have the opposite effect to what you intended? Why?

Lighting

32

Stage lighting is the use of artificial light to create a range of effects and moods, or to direct the audience's attention.

Lights are usually classified as either **spotlights**, which can be controlled and moved quite easily to follow a character around the stage, or **floodlights**, which create a general, more widespread light and tend to be set in one position.

Key terms
- **spotlight**
- **floodlight**

An actor under a spotlight in a production of The Four Alice Bakers *by Fay Weldon at the Birmingham Repertory Theatre*

A scene lit with floodlights in a production of Speed the Plow *by David Mamet, Starring Kevin Spacey at the Old Vic Theatre*

Successful stage lighting

Good stage lighting creates the environment in which the drama takes place, but does not dominate it. It illuminates what is on stage, allowing the audience to see what is happening. It can also:

- direct the audience's attention to a particular part of the stage or scenery
- create the tone or mood (for example, a soft, pale light will have a different effect from a fiery red one)
- suggest time and place (for example, night and day or indoor and outdoor location)
- signal a change in the plot or action (for example, by changing to introduce a new event or character).

Lighting can be a complex and challenging part of productions and it is important to know what can be achieved with all the different sorts of lamps and lights available.

edexcel examiner tip
Remember that lighting doesn't have to involve elaborate technical equipment. You can also achieve good effects with standard lighting, small lamps and torches. Make sure you pay attention to all health and safety issues.

There are some good effects that can be achieved even with the most basic lamps or lighting.

For example:

Action	Effect
Cutting the lights suddenly	Brings an abrupt, sudden end to a piece of drama or scene.
Fade up lights gradually	Introduces us slowly to a new scene – might suggest the passing of time, or a new situation.
Bright full lighting (usually a floodlight if you are using proper stage lighting)	Can suggest daytime, outdoor light and sunlight.
Fade down lighting	Signifies the end of a scene but not necessarily in a dramatic manner. This could be as a character leaves the acting area to 'move on' to the next moment in the play.
Lower level, weaker lighting	Can be used to convey darkness, evening or a gloomy interior scene. Take care that you don't underlight the scene. In general terms, it is better to have too much light than too little. It is no good if the audience can't see what is going on.

Try it!

Take on the role of lighting designer. Read the opening lines of the play below. Imagine what the set is like. The play takes place close to the forest so the set design will suggest this.

Make notes about:

- how you might direct the audience's attention using lights
- what colours you might use and why.

> The STORYTELLER *enters and speaks to the audience.*
>
> STORYTELLER: Once, long ago, in the early days of the world, before stories had ever come into the world, there was a boy who lived with his grandmother.
>
> (*The* BOY *and the* GRANDMOTHER *enter. The* GRANDMOTHER *carries a bow and some arrows.*)
>
> The boy's father and mother were dead, and he only had his grandmother to care for him in all the world, and she only had him. One day, the grandmother said to the boy…
>
> GRANDMOTHER: You must go into the forest to get food. If you don't hunt, we'll starve.
>
> STORYTELLER: And she gave the boy the bow and arrows that had belonged to his father.
>
> From *Gifts of Flame* by David Calcutt

Evaluation

Show your lighting decisions to a partner and compare your ideas with his or hers.

- Were any of your ideas the same? If not, which do you think might be most effective, and why?
- What effects were you each trying to convey?
- Do you think you succeeded?

Space and levels

Space means the area between and around the actors themselves but also the space in which the drama takes place. For example, there is usually space between the audience and actors, as well as the space created by the stage and surroundings.

The levels used by actors within the space – for example, high and low – can affect the way we see characters and their relationships.

Successful use of space and levels

Use of space and levels should:

- fit the drama. For example, a psychological thriller with two characters might work best in a small, dark and confined space

- create interesting effects, for example, when one character is on a higher level than another and cannot be seen by him or her

- add meaning to a performance. For example, a simple spoken line between two characters can change in significance depending on how they are positioned in relation to each other – close, far apart, above or below each other, or with obstacles between them.

The balcony scene from a production of Shakesphere's Romeo and Juliet *at the National Theatre*

Try it!

Work in threes. Two will be actors and the third will observe and direct.

First, learn this very simple dialogue:

A: There you are.

B: Yes.

A: I got held up.

B: So I see.

A: Do you want a coffee or something?

B: No, I'm fine thanks.

Now, perform the dialogue three times, each with a different use of space, as outlined below. Try to keep your voices the same in each version (e.g. don't be angry in one and then calm in the other).

- A and B remain far apart throughout the dialogue – perhaps on either side of the acting space. C (the director) can decide whether they face each other or whether A or B has his/her back turned.

- A and B stand very close to each other – perhaps facing each other, half a metre apart.

- The space between A and B changes throughout the dialogue (as directed by C). For example, begin far apart, then come closer.

34

Evaluation

After the three versions have been tried, discuss the effects of the different uses of space.

- Was the first more cold or distant?
- How did the changing use of space in the third option affect how those watching saw the relationship?
- What other uses of space could you have introduced?

Try it!

Now try the same dialogue in your threes again but swap roles, so that different people are playing A, B and C. Use a chair to experiment with different levels.

Take turns at deciding how the chair will be used, when and by whom. What is the effect if, for example, B remains seated throughout? What is the effect if A comes in and sits down straight away?

Staging terms

Make sure you are familiar with the staging terms linked to space and levels. Use the diagram below to help you. It shows a stage from above. Note that left and right are from the actors' perspective when on stage, facing the audience.

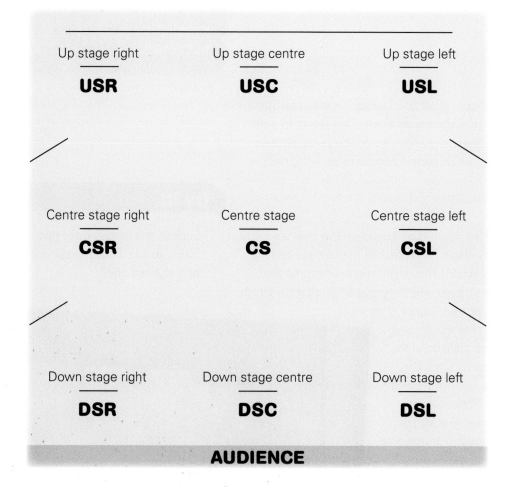

| Up stage right | Up stage centre | Up stage left |
| **USR** | **USC** | **USL** |

| Centre stage right | Centre stage | Centre stage left |
| **CSR** | **CS** | **CSL** |

| Down stage right | Down stage centre | Down stage left |
| **DSR** | **DSC** | **DSL** |

AUDIENCE

Set and props

The set is the constructed or created setting in which a play takes place. A set can be as simple as a couple of chairs, or as detailed as a magical forest with castles, trees and trap-doors. The set can change during a performance, for example, at the end of a scene or act.

The props are the items used by an actor in his or her performance, such as a murderer's dagger, a letter or a cup and saucer.

What makes a successful set?

An effective set:

- forms part of the overall design and vision of the director, producer or actors. It can have symbolic power and convey important messages about the story
- can convince an audience that they are inside another time and place, or even world
- is safe and easy for the actors to perform in.

Styles of set

Sets tend to fall into one of two categories:

- Realistic/naturalistic
- Stylised.

Realistic/naturalistic set

A **realistic** set attempts to present what you see as if it was real life, for example, someone's lounge, a garden or a café. This tends to work when there is a location that doesn't change much. The term 'kitchen sink drama' refers to drama in which people appear to be living ordinary lives in quite everyday places.

Stylised set

A **stylised** set aims to create an impression based on the themes and relationships within a play rather than pretend that we are looking through a window at the 'real world'. This might mean using modern furniture for old fairy tales, or strange, abstract shapes and forms which don't look like 'real' buildings or landscapes. It might also mean using 'minimalist' sets – with very few objects (perhaps a chair or table only) to suggest the setting.

The amount of information that playwrights provide about sets varies. Some give lots of detailed information in their scripts; others may describe the overall scene but not the detail. Some contain only the minimum of information about the setting.

> **Key terms**
> - realistic
> - stylised

> **Try it!**
>
> Look at this image. Does this strike you as a naturalistic set or a stylised one?

Here is the opening to Act 1, Scene 1 of Charlotte Jones' play, *Humble Boy*.

Set: a pretty country garden. Perhaps the suggestions of a house or a glass conservatory from which the characters enter into the garden. A patio area, perhaps with a path through the garden. At the back there is an area for gardening tools: a gardening chair or stool. There is a garden hosepipe wound up there. Something of a lawn with borders. A rose bush. At the end of the garden there is a large beehive. The suggestion of an apple tree perhaps just some overhanging branches with a few apples.

Does the above sound more like a stylised or naturalistic set? Could it be either? How could you suggest the garden without showing everything described here?

Sometimes, designers describe their vision for the set. On the right, an RSC set designer describes the set for a production of *Romeo and Juliet* by William Shakespeare.

Two vast, curved, lattice walls of stone and metal move about the stage to form orchard walls, the balcony, the banquet hall; in the second half they cast grid-like shadows and become walls of the tomb itself. The Friar's hut is built with corrugated iron like a shanty-town shack, an Aladdin's cave of potions, herbs and books. Props on the whole are sparse and serve several functions; Romeo kills Paris with the 'mattock' (a kind of pick-axe) he has brought to force open the tomb.

Try it!

Create a larger version of the diagram to the right and using either the description of the opening scene of *Humble Boy*, or another drama of your choice, draw a set design. Think carefully about the style of your set. A stylised or minimalist one would take a few objects and ideas and represent them simply. A naturalistic one would look as realistic as possible.

Annotate your diagram to explain your choices for the drama, or make notes below it.

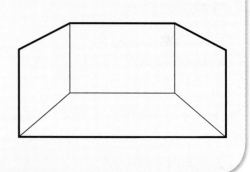

Evaluation

Discuss the advantages and disadvantages of realistic and stylised sets. Think about:

- believability
- cost
- ease of use for actors on stage
- flexibility.

Independent research

Look at the beginning of these plays to see what information was provided by the playwright about the setting:

- William Shakespeare's *Macbeth*
- Caryl Churchill's *Top Girls*
- Henrik Ibsen's *A Doll's House*

Remember to check what details the playwright has given for the play you will study in Unit 2. There is an image of a set design for Arthur Miller's play *The Crucible* on page 140.

To give you an idea of the range of possible set designs, it might help to look at designs on the RSC website (www.rsc.org.uk) or the National Theatre Stagework website (www.stagework.org).

Movement, mime and gesture

Movement is all the physical action that happens on stage, including both individual physical actions and the overall action of groups (for example, in a fight scene).

Mime is a dramatic technique in which the actors remain silent and convey meaning through actions.

Gesture is a single movement, made by part of the body, such as a fist clenching, or hands nervously adjusting a tie.

Successful use of movement or gesture

Effective use of movement or gesture:

- contributes to our understanding of character (for example, a conman winking at the audience before he fools his next victim)
- fits the mood or action of a scene (for example, a mob waving their fists and surging forward to confront an unpopular ruler).

Who decides how an actor moves?

The **playwright** sometimes indicates how an actor should move or gesture in the play-script. Note the clues in the opening scene of *Humble Boy* by Charlotte Jones.

> Mercy Lott enters the garden. She is wearing black clothes with brown shoes. She is in her late fifties, a petite and timid, mousy woman. She watches Felix with concern. She approaches him, but doesn't get too close. Felix glances at her, then returns his attention to the hive.

The **director** often has a vision of how he or she wants characters to move. These are the notes of a youth theatre director working on a piece of drama about gang relationships and bullying.

> I wanted the gang to be like a pack of animals - very physical, rough, with the sense that any moment violent emotions could come through - whether these were anger, love, hate, jealousy etc, so that's why they move as one, on the prowl.

The **actor** usually has strong ideas about how his or her character might move and behave. Anthony Sher played Iago in *Othello*, and describes how he imagines his physical contact with others.

> I have an image of him being very tactile and touching people a lot whatever their sex and sexuality. I think the reason why he can use jealousy as such a weapon is because he suffers from it himself very, very badly. Jealousy in the play isn't just what is put on to Othello - it is the poison inside.

Movement can be broken down into different areas. Look at the mind map below and think carefully about what each term means.

Walking
How can different styles of walking express different moods or character, e.g. long confident strides, reluctant shuffling, rhythmic plodding?

Angle
How might the position of an actor affect how the audience sees him or her? For example, standing 'side on' partly hides the face so might suit a trickster character.

Gesture (body and limbs)
How might everyday actions, such as shaking hands or putting on a jacket, express something about character? What can single gestures, like a wave or hug, reveal about character?

Movement

Posture
How might a character stand, e.g. crouched over, head up, very straight-backed? How might this reflect their role and mood?

Gesture (face)
How can different facial expressions reflect different characters and their moods, e.g. the weariness of an elderly character? How can eye movements convey feelings and relationships, e.g. fluttering eyelashes, staring, glancing?

Speed/pace
How quickly might a character make a gesture or move across the stage? How can their speed influence our opinion of them?

Try it!

Create a character through mime. Choose one of the following and devise a simple sequence of movements for your character to move across your performance space.

| A soldier on patrol in a foreign jungle | A little child on his or her first day at infant school | A teenager joking around on a visit to a zoo |

Think carefully about:

- how your clothing might affect your movement, e.g. a heavy coat, high shoes, a tight jacket
- what you might be carrying, e.g. a gun or a lollipop.

Remember, your mime should be soundless!

Evaluation

◉ How successfully were each character's movements conveyed?

◉ Which was most difficult and why?

Try it!

Now apply similar ideas to characters from a script. Working with a partner, read the script below and experiment with the way the characters enter and how they act. From your character's perspective, say how you would move and why, making reference to the text.

Scene: Ryan's bedroom

Ryan's mother is sitting on his bed. She is looking at his diary. **She is ...**
Enter Ryan. **He is ...**

RYAN: What are you doing? Give that to me.

MUM: I....I....

RYAN: Spit it out!

MUM: Don't be cross. I was tidying your bed when...

RYAN: It fell into your hands?

MUM: Yes...no, of course not. It's just...well, I've been worried. Dad too.

RYAN: So that gives you the right to go nosing through my belongings?

MUM: No – of course not. It was wrong of me.

RYAN: Yes.

MUM: Look – I'll go. But...if you want to talk...

RYAN: Shut the door on your way out.

Evaluation

◉ What did your ideas for movement convey about the characters?

◉ What ideas did others in the class have?

◉ How would different suggestions for movement affect how the audience sees the characters?

Voice

> Voice refers to the various ways you alter your voice as an actor to convey feeling and expression.

Successful use of voice

The use of voice can be broken down into different areas which you will need to consider: volume, pitch, stress, accent and tone.

Volume

How loudly or quietly we say something on stage can change its meaning. You need to think carefully about the use of volume because the most obvious levels of sound are not always the most effective. For example, a quiet and intense voice might express extreme anger more effectively than loud shouting. All actors need to project their voice (make it carry over distance) so that the audience can hear.

Pitch

Pitch is like the higher and lower notes on the piano. Some people have a high-pitched voice (generally children); others have a lower-pitched voice. To some extent, we can change the pitch of our voices. This variation of pitch is called intonation and can reflect a changing mood or attitude. For example, a parent might scold a child in a deep voice and then switch to a higher pitch when they find out that the child isn't the culprit after all.

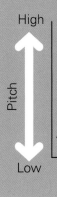

High

Pitch

wasn't

Oh – so it   you who spilled the milk!

You've been very naughty, haven't you?

Low

42

Stress

Stress is the particular weight we give to individual words or phrases. Where we put the stress in a line can change its meaning. Repeat the following line aloud, putting the stress on different words or phrases each time to explore the different meanings:

Marcia saw Dan hiding in the garden.

Accent

Accent is the characteristic sound of a voice according to region, nationality or social class.

Tone

This is the overall quality, strength and pitch of a voice, which reflects the attitude or mood of a character. For example, a spiteful tone might be used towards Cinderella by a cruel sister.

Try it!

Work in pairs on the following line:

I regret so much that I married that old fool!

Repeat it aloud and try applying each of the following techniques to it:

- Choose different words to stress.
- Alter the volume.
- Change the pitch.
- Try out a variety of tones and accents.

Discuss what effect each of these techniques has. What do they tell you about the meaning of the words and the person who says them?

Try it!

The text below comes from the play *The School for Scandal* by Sheridan. In this monologue, an elderly gentleman, Sir Peter Teazle, regrets that he married a young wife from the country. Read it aloud, ensuring you sound each word separately. Don't worry if it sounds artificial at this point. The purpose of the task is to practise using your voice, rather like a muscle or limb.

SIR PETER:
When an old bachelor marries a young wife, what is he to expect? 'Tis now six months since Lady Teazle made me the happiest of men—and I have been the most miserable dog ever since! We tift a little going to church, and fairly quarrelled before the bells had done ringing. I was more than once nearly choked with gall during the honeymoon, and had lost all comfort in life before my friends had done wishing me joy. Yet I chose with caution—a girl bred wholly in the country, who never knew luxury beyond one silk gown, nor dissipation above the annual gala of a race ball. Yet she now plays her part in all the extravagant fopperies of fashion and the town, with as ready a grace as if she never had seen a bush or a grass-plot out of Grosvenor Square! I am sneered at by all my acquaintance, and paragraphed in the newspapers. She dissipates my fortune, and contradicts all my humours; yet the worst of it is, I doubt I love her*, or I should never bear all this. However, I'll never be weak enough to own it.

Sir Peter Teazle and his wife in a touring production of School for Scandal.

* *I doubt I love her*: Today, we might express this idea by using the word 'fear' instead of 'doubt'. Sir Peter is saying that he loves his wife and that is why he puts up with her behaviour and its consequences.

Once you are familiar with the text, decide which words or phrases you will emphasise, or how your voice will change. Think also about tone and accent.

Evaluation

Listen to all members of your group speak the monologue, then discuss the performances.

⦿ Were some speeches funny or sad? If so, why?

⦿ Did particular words or phrases stand out more in one version than another?

⦿ Did anyone have a particularly clear voice? Did they sound natural? Why?

⦿ Who, in your opinion, made the character of Sir Peter come alive most through their voice skills? How?

⦿ What did you learn about your own performance and your own voice as an actor?

Spoken language

Spoken language refers to the choice of words used in drama. The choice of words can convey specific ideas about the characters, plot and themes.

In drama, language can be used in different forms and styles:

Monologue
A form of language which is a long speech by one actor, often alone on stage.

Dialogue
A form of speech which is between two or more characters.

Poetic language
A style of language that has a strong sense of sound and rhythm and is often in verse.

Prosaic language
A style of language that is used in a functional way on a daily basis.

Successful spoken language

Successful spoken language:

- fits the character or drama
- has emotional, comic or descriptive power or significance
- can create meaning through one word, one phrase or one line.

Try it!

In pairs, rehearse both versions of the dialogue below.

Version 1

CHRIS: I've been waiting here by the school gate for ages. Where on earth did you get to? Did you forget what we're supposed to be doing?

JULIE: Sorry. I got held up – you know, usual stuff at home. Anyway, I'm here now, so are we going to go, or what?

Version 2

CHRIS: Where did you get to?

JULIE: I got held up. So, are we going then?

Is there a difference in meaning between the two extracts? Talk about:

- which version has most words and whether it gives more information
- which version leaves 'space for meaning' (i.e. leaves room for the audience and actors to add their own interpretation).

Poetry and prose

Poetic or rhythmic choices of language add another aspect to a performance. Read aloud the extract below from Shakespeare's *The Tempest*. These words are spoken by Ariel, a magical spirit.

> *Full fathom five, thy father lies*
> *Of his bones, are coral made*
> *Those are pearls that were his eyes.*

Now read the second version aloud.

> *Deep below the water's surface your dad lies*
> *His bones are made of coral now*
> *His eyes have been turned into pearls*

Think carefully about what is lost by changing the word order and the choice of some of the words.

- How has the sound of the extract changed?
- Are there still patterns in the language?
- Which version do you think best suits a magical character?

Choosing appropriate language

Choosing words suited to your character and situation is important.

Think about what sort of background and education your character might have had. However, try to avoid **stereotyping**. For example, a character who is a night cleaner in a block of flats could also be a student training to be a nuclear physicist or lawyer by day. Some of the most interesting improvisations reveal some unexpected twists for the audience.

Think carefully about your vocabulary (choice of individual words). The English language provides many different ways of saying similar things.

Cyndia Sieden playing Ariel in a production of The Tempest at the Royal Opera House in London

Key terms
- **stereotyping**

Try it!

1. Look carefully at all the words in the panel. They are very similar in meaning.

   wet   moist   soaked   drenched   sodden   dripping   damp   permeated

   Which of these words would suit the following characters and situations?
   - A forensic scientist inspecting some material from a crime
   - A snake in a myth describing the bark of a tree where it lives
   - A mother telling her child to come in out of the rain.

2. Improvise a short scene in which a police officer interrogates a teenager about a stolen car. Think carefully about the choice of words for each character and how much dialogue to use. Remember, fewer words can often have as much or greater impact than many.

Evaluation

What choices did you make about what language to use? Why?

Elements of Drama
Action, plot and content

The action of a play is the events that unfold before the audience.

The play's action is usually divided up into acts and scenes. The action includes:

- the main plot (the key storyline)
- sub-plots (less important stories that run alongside the main plot).

The action makes up the main content of the play, and is driven by what the characters do.

See the grid below for some examples and add your own.

The main plot	Example of sub-plot/s
In *The Tempest*, an exiled Duke and his daughter take revenge on the people who mistreated them, when these people are shipwrecked on their island.	*The Duke's slave joins up with two shipwrecked sailors to try to overthrow him.*
In *The Crucible*, a group of young women are accused of witchcraft. Their 'confessions' of devil worship lead to the wrongful imprisonment of and accusations against members of their community.	*One of the farmers in the community is trying to mend his marriage with his wife after an affair with one of the young women accused of witchcraft.*

Important factors in plot and action

- *Revealing the story:* The play may start in the middle of the story with the audience learning about previous events through **cross-cutting**. For example, in *The Tempest* we learn about how Prospero came to the island through his conversation with his daughter Miranda.
- *Plot progression:* Some playwrights unravel a plot in a slow and roundabout way to add tension and suspense and avoid predictability. For example, in *The Tempest*, Prospero remains hidden from his enemies as he allows them to suffer, rather than revealing himself straight away.
- *Events off stage:* The story which unravels on stage often depends on something that the audience does not see. The 'unseen' events may later be revealed to the audience through many different drama mediums including movement, spoken language, costume or props.
- *Individual sub-plots:* Characters develop their own individual stories within the main plot, each with their own motivations, goals and resolutions. For example, in *The Tempest* everyone is on the same island, but each character has a different motive (to survive, to get revenge, to marry someone they love, etc.)

Try it!

Use prompts like these to explore how plot and action work in your own drama.

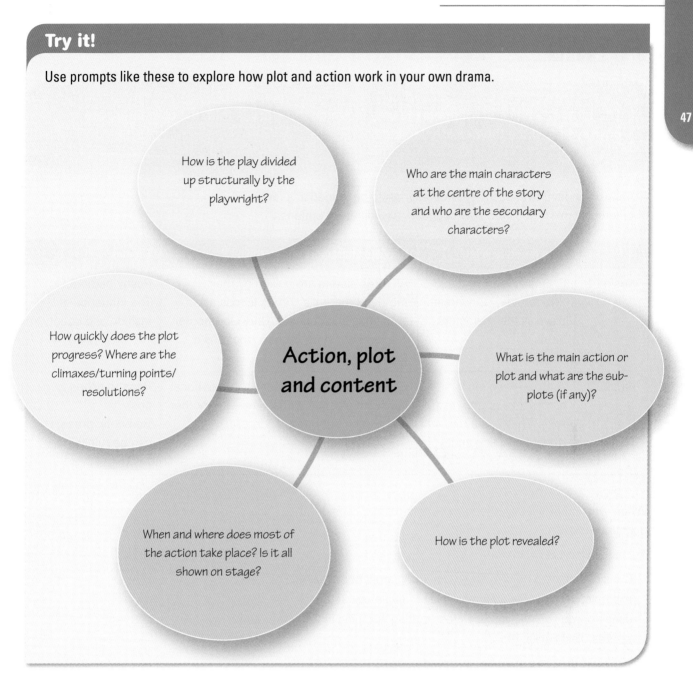

How is the play divided up structurally by the playwright?

Who are the main characters at the centre of the story and who are the secondary characters?

How quickly does the plot progress? Where are the climaxes/turning points/resolutions?

Action, plot and content

What is the main action or plot and what are the sub-plots (if any)?

When and where does most of the action take place? Is it all shown on stage?

How is the plot revealed?

Evaluation

Discuss the information you have gathered about the plot/content of your play. Use the following questions to start your discussion:

- What effect would the action have on an audience? Is the play exciting, thoughtful, reflective, humorous or full of suspense? Perhaps it's a mix.

- What do you think are the main themes of the play, based on the plot and action that are present? Give reasons for your ideas.

Forms

48

> The form of a piece of drama is the way in which the story is told, the characters are portrayed and the themes are depicted.

A well-known fairy tale, such as *Cinderella*, could be staged in a range of different forms. The grid below suggests two different options.

	How the story is told	How the characters are portrayed	Themes
Version 1	Dramatic monologue. 'Modern day' Cinderella plays all the characters herself.	All three sisters are bullied by their mother. Cinderella comes across as ambitious and cunning. Fairy Godmother is a local businesswoman who runs a fashion agency.	Pushy parents. The influence of fashion and beauty.
Version 2	A group of young actors take on the main roles. They use a mix of dance, acting and songs.	Characters are portrayed in the traditional way with a conventional Fairy Godmother and a poor, put-upon Cinderella.	Rags to riches is possible. Romantic dreams can be fulfilled.

When working to develop the form of your drama, consider the questions below.

- How will you tell the story?

  Consider all the different ways your story could be revealed. For example, will you use a narrator, play multiple characters or use dance or music? Will you use cross-cutting (jumping in time between scenes, flashbacks, etc.)?

- How will the characters be portrayed?

  Consider the range of interpretations for your characters. For example, will you have recognisable 'types', or will your characters act in surprising ways? What will their motivations be? How will their stories end? How will they behave and appear?

- What will your themes be?

  Consider what themes are important within your play. Your drama may seem to have one obvious issue or theme but think carefully about how you will explore this. You may want to say something fresh and unusual about this theme, or even introduce a new one!

Try it!

Working with a partner add your own suggestions about the forms that could be used to stage *Cinderella* or another well-known fairytale.

Climax and anti-climax

The climax of a play or drama is when a sense of expectation is built up and the story and action reach their most critical point. Feelings spill over and tension is released.

Anti-climax is when there has been the same sort of build-up but the key moment doesn't come. Alternatively, the outcome is less serious, or delayed.

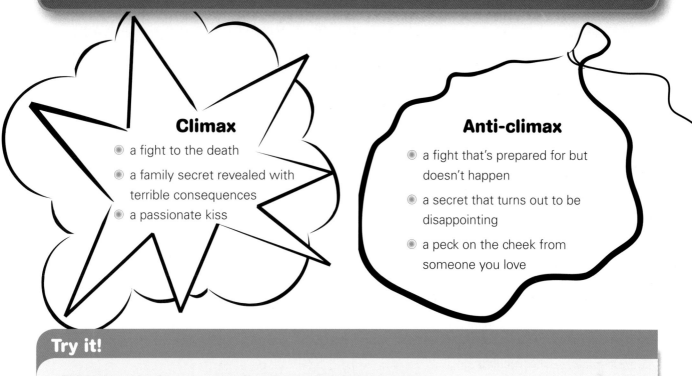

Climax

- a fight to the death
- a family secret revealed with terrible consequences
- a passionate kiss

Anti-climax

- a fight that's prepared for but doesn't happen
- a secret that turns out to be disappointing
- a peck on the cheek from someone you love

Try it!

Think about any drama you are directing, performing or creating:

- Is there a climax in it? If not, why not? Should there be one?
- Where is the climax or anti-climax and what is its function? For example, to include a moment of great danger or, in the case of anti-climax, perhaps to create a comic moment for the audience.
- How does the drama build up to it?
- What effect does it have on the characters and the story that follows?
- What happens afterwards?

Evaluation

You can check the position of the climax in your drama by plotting the tension on a graph. The climax should come after a gradual rise in tension in previous scenes. The tension reduces immediately after the climax.

Try to pinpoint the exact lines within the drama when the tension builds up, as well as the exact point at which the climax or anti-climax occurs. You can then write these lines alongside the appropriate place on a graph like this one.

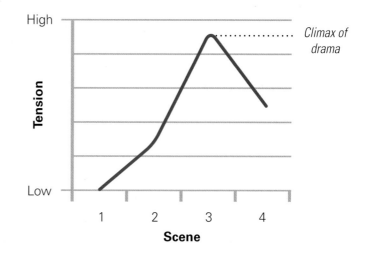

Rhythm, pace and tempo

The rhythm, pace and tempo of a piece of drama involve the speed at which the action moves along and how this changes. Changes in rhythm, pace and tempo are also reflected in speech.

Here's an example of varying pace in a short drama.

Scene	Action in the play	Rhythm, pace and tempo
Scene 1	Short, busy activities. Lots of characters coming and going. Short, sharp lines reflecting bursts of physical action.	Uneven rhythm and a swift pace and tempo.
Scene 2	Single character on stage reflects on the past – slower speech with little or no movement.	Steady rhythm. Slow pace and tempo.
Scene 3	Two characters burst in, arguing, then calm down. There are loud, sharp bursts of speech, matching the energetic physical entrance, but reducing to slower, calmer speech later on.	The tempo starts off fast, with high energy, but the scene slows into an even rhythm, pace and tempo as it progresses.
Scene 4	Same character from Scene 2 quietly summarises what has happened. Slow, deliberate speech, reflecting little or no movement.	There is a steady rhythm to this speech with a slow pace and minimum change in tempo.

Try it!

Reflect on how you might use varying pace and tempo in your work. Think about the patterns and variations of rhythm:

- **within a scene** – a scene can change from being busy and active to slower and more focused
- **within a speech** – an angry character can start a speech full of passion and emotion but end it being thoughtful and quiet
- **between characters** – one could be agitated in speech and movement, pacing around the stage, while the other is quieter and stands still
- **between scenes** – the pace and style of an opening scene may be echoed in a closing scene.

Contrasts

Contrasts are created when opposites are put together to produce a specific effect or impression. Contrasts can occur between things that are directly seen or heard (for example, stillness versus activity or speech versus silence), or in the play as a whole, such as contrasts in location, theme or characterisation.

Successful contrasts

These can be:

- between scenes or acts – a happy love scene followed by an angry or tragic one

- between characters – a son who makes his father proud and a different son in another family who makes his family ashamed

- between location and atmosphere – a dark, interior evening scene in a city followed by daylight and a rural scene outside

- between different uses of language – a character who uses informal, chatty, friendly speech, and a character who speaks formally and coldly.

Try it!

Read and perform the short extract below. As you do so, try to draw out the different contrasts, thinking carefully what they reveal about the characters and the situation.

Scene 1: Jo's kitchen

Jo sitting at table, head in her hands, says nothing. Jo's mother paces the room, anxiously checks mobile and looks out of the window:

JO'S MOTHER: When's he going to call? I mean, it's been four hours. Four hours! Where's he got to ... the stupid, stupid boy. *(She breaks off and looks at Jo.)* Say something, Jo – please!

Jo looks up, but remains seated.

Evaluation

- What contrasts did you create? Think about what could be heard as well as seen within the scene.

- What effect did the contrasts have on the audience? Were they simply to add interest or were they central to the story (for example, two daughters who behave in entirely different ways, leading to a powerful climax of emotion)?

Characterisation

Characterisation is the creation of convincing, believable characters using a range of techniques and skills. For example, the way you use your voice, your gestures and your movement in a role.

Successful characterisation

Good characterisation uses what you know about a character to help portray the role effectively. It involves:

- having a thorough insight into, and understanding of, the role
- your ability to draw on a range of techniques to create your character
- your ability to sustain the role (stay in character).

The stages outlined below show how you can prepare for a successful characterisation.

David Tennant playing the lead role in Hamlet *with the Royal Shakespeare Company*

STAGE 1: What do I know about my character?

- What does my character look like? What do I wear?
- What do I know about his/her relationships?
- What is my character's motive in the drama?
- What does my character say and do?
- What do others say about my character?
- How do others behave towards my character?

STAGE 2: How would my character move?

- Does my character tend to move quickly, slowly, smoothly, clumsily?
- Does my character use large gestures, or smaller ones?
- Does my character have a particular gesture or habit that he/she repeats?
- Does my character move differently when he/she is with different characters?

STAGE 3: How would my character speak and use his/her voice?

- Does my character tend to speak quickly, slowly?
- Does my character have a particular vocal feature (e.g. a lisp)?
- Does my character speak differently when he/she is with different characters?
- What tone of voice does my character have – deep, rough, sarcastic?
- Does my character have particular words or phrases that he/she repeats?

Try it!

Read this short script and choose one of the characters. Then work with a partner and go through the different stages (on page 52) to practise characterisation. Continue to improvise the scene, staying in role as much as possible.

The following scene takes place in the canteen of a young offenders' institution on an island. An inspector (older man/woman) is wondering where all the staff are. In fact, there has been a sort of rebellion led by 'the ringleader'.

INSPECTOR: What is going on here?

RINGLEADER: Nothing.

INSPECTOR: Nothing?

RINGLEADER: Nothing much – you can see that everything is fine.

INSPECTOR: Everything *looks* fine.

RINGLEADER: Exactly.

INSPECTOR: But it's not fine – is it? Where are the staff?

From *Hope Springs* by Richard Conlon

Evaluation

- How did you create your character? How did you bring him/her alive?
- Were there any moments in the dialogue when you used a specific gesture (e.g. a hand on the shoulder) or a movement (e.g. turning your back)? If so, why?
- How did you decide to speak? What tone of voice did you use? Why?

Now think about any drama you are currently working on. What could you do to develop your characterisation? Use the grid below to help.

Gesture and movement	What effect would this have?
I could raise one eyebrow.	This would show disbelief and suspicion in the role of the inspector.
Voice and speech	**What effect would this have?**
I could have a slow pace and even tone to my voice.	This would give the impression that I am trying to reassure the inspector and convince him that everything is normal.

Conventions

Conventions are the techniques that are typically used in drama performance and development work. These help you to explore and portray character, themes, issues and the plot/action of the play.

Examples of typical drama conventions are:

- use of slow motion (e.g. to show a speedy physical event that could not be imitated on stage)

- still image (holding the action to capture a moment)

- audience asides (when a character has a 'private' word with the audience, while other characters are on stage)

- **soliloquy** (a character speaking their thoughts while on their own on stage)

- dividing the stage to show more than one location at a time.

These conventions are used by performers, designers and audiences when preparing, performing or watching a drama. Understanding and being able to draw upon a range of conventions will help you to create original and compelling drama.

Key terms
- soliloquy

Try it!

Consider a simple story:

- A villager is sent to take a written message to a king in a faraway land.
- Along the way the villager experiences many dangers and challenges, such as a violent storm, and being set upon by thieves.
- The villager loses the message, much to his/her distress.
- After many hardships, he/she arrives at the palace and apologises to the king.
- The king forgives the villager and says it was a test – there was no message.
- The villager is rewarded for his/her honesty and determination.

Choose any part of the plot and decide what conventions you could use and the effect they would create.

Plot development	Convention to use	The effect of the convention
The attack by thieves	Slow motion	This would slow down the events to show how the villager was tricked and then beaten. It would emphasise this crucial event and make it dramatically powerful.
The villager's concern at losing the message		

Symbols

A symbol is a recurring object or image that represents a theme or idea within a piece of drama.

In drama, symbols are used to represent ideas or feelings and can be any of the following:

- items such as props or costumes
- character behaviour such as expressions or gestures
- stage elements such as lighting or setting.

Symbols are a quick way of communicating ideas without having to explain what they mean. The best use of symbols comes when they arise naturally from the action of the drama and the main themes of the play.

Try it!

Match the symbols listed below to what they might represent. The pairs are currently in the wrong order.

Symbol	The effect of the symbol
A doll's house (also the title of the play).	The appearance of a character who is out to get revenge for the murder of his father when he was a child. The father was forced to play a musical instrument as he was tortured.
A woman sleepwalking and washing her hands again and again.	A young man with a good future ahead of him goes missing for several years after his plane crashed in the war.
The sound of a harmonica playing the same eerie melody.	A play about a woman whose husband treats her like a child.
An apple tree on stage in a garden, half-destroyed in a storm.	A play about a murderess who is haunted by the guilt of her bloody crimes.

Evaluation

- Why is the use of each symbol effective? How does it emphasise a key theme or idea? How do the characters within the play relate to the symbol or what it represents? How does it affect the mood of the play for the audience?

Independent research

Find out more about the use of symbol in one of the three plays or the film referred to here. They are:

Once Upon a Time in the West by film director Sergio Leone
All My Sons by Arthur Miller
A Doll's House by Henrik Ibsen
Macbeth by William Shakespeare

- Are there any themes or ideas in your own drama which you could highlight through use of a recurring symbol in a similar way? What symbol would be appropriate for your drama and why?

Forms of Stimuli

Stimuli are various things that can stimulate – or create – ideas for drama. Your teacher will provide you with the stimuli for your exploration in Unit 1 and the play script you explore in Unit 2. You may also be devising drama from a stimulus in Unit 3.

Some examples of stimuli are:

- poems
- artefacts (this means objects such as photos, pictures, masks, props, costume, sculpture or other art objects)
- music
- play scripts
- live theatre performances
- television, film, radio, DVD, video, the web, etc.
- newspaper and magazine articles
- extracts from literary fiction and non-fiction.

The stimuli will offer you and your class the chance to:

- be creative. They will allow you to think outside your day-to-day sphere – a school uniform, a bowl of cereal and a homework diary will most likely not be involved!
- develop ideas. You may get fragments, unfinished business, missing endings, mysteries and the like, which will be easier to develop than complete accounts or sources.
- explore meaning. You may have everyday objects as your stimuli but these can still prompt you to ask questions that you should try to find the answers to within your drama work.
- make connections between different stimuli to help you reflect on the topics, themes or issues that they introduce.

How you might use your stimuli

The following examples will help you to understand how you can use explorative strategies to explore a topic, theme or issue in response to a set of stimuli.

Example 1: Fame

Imagine that you are exploring the topic of fame. Your teacher shows you a photograph of Tiger Woods and plays you the title song from the musical, *Fame*. Some of the possibilities for drama work in response to these might be:

- **still image** showing a moment of glory and leading to a sound collage

- a **hot-seating** exercise on the pressures of fame

- **role-play** with 'fame' interviewing 'failure'

- **cross-cutting** between the fantasy of fame and the reality of fame.

Example 2: Environment

Now imagine that you arrive for your drama lesson to find your studio vandalised. Your teacher gives you *We Are Going to See the Rabbit* by Alan Brownjohn, a poem about the last rabbit in England disappearing. These stimuli might lead you to explore what it would be like if no one cared about anything or anyone, for example, by:

- **role-playing** a meeting of two people who representorder and disorder to see what imposes order on disorder

- your teacher **narrating** a description of a landscape while your class responds by becoming features of the landscape

- **thought-tracking** in role about what has happened to the landscape.

How do I use stimuli successfully?

1. Ask questions about the stimuli. For example, you might ask the following questions about an object:

   - Where does it come from?

   - How would I describe it?

   - Where might it be found?

   - Does it have a story attached to it?

   - Who owns it – if anyone?

   - What could it stand for (i.e. does it have a meaning, like a wedding ring)? If it's a work of art, what did the artist want to express through the work?

2. Allow your ideas and those of your group, which result from the stimuli, to follow several paths and possibilities, but be prepared to cut this number down later to use just a few that you can really develop.

3. The foundation of drama is the way in which a story is told. Keep this in mind with whatever stimuli you are given.

Unit 1: Drama Exploration

What will you do in Unit 1?

- Use stimulus material as a starting point to explore a theme, topic or issue. You will make use of the explorative strategies, drama medium and elements of drama to create your own work and communicate meaning

- Evaluate how your exploration and use of techniques contribute to your creation of drama.

How are you assessed in Unit 1?

Unit 1 is worth a total of **30%** of your GCSE marks.

20% of your marks will be for a six-hour assessed practical exploration of drama. This may take place on one day or be spread over a number of shorter sessions. It will take place under controlled conditions, led, supervised and assessed by your teacher.

In this exploration you will use at least two stimuli, four explorative strategies and two examples of the drama medium from the Programme of Study. There will also be opportunities to use the elements of drama. You will do a lot of other drama work for Unit 1 to prepare you for this six-hour assessment.

The remaining **10%** of the marks will be for a documentary response recording the work you have undertaken in Unit 1. This is based on notes made during and after the exploration and can include photographs, sketches and diagrams as well as writing. It should be no more than 2,000 words and will be written under controlled conditions, with supervision.

How will this book help you with Unit 1?

In this section there are five explorations, using a range of stimuli. Each exploration covers more work than you will do in the six-hour assessed practical exploration: your teacher will select the activities you will work on and the ones that may be used for the assessed exploration. In most instances the stimulus material is supplied. Where the stimulus includes film, music or the internet, your teacher will need to provide it.

Remember that you may explore a different topic, theme or issue from the ones covered here. If so, you can still use the examples that follow to help you understand how to make use of explorative strategies, drama medium and elements of drama within Unit 1. For example, the Try it! boxes suggest how you can use a stimulus to create imaginative drama. and you can apply these ideas to your own exploration. Your teacher will help you to pick the examples which you can adapt to suit your work.

How do you use the Programme of Study in Unit 1?

The example below offers one possible way of applying the Programme of Study in a Unit 1 practical exploration. The fuller exploration projects that follow in this unit will help you to extend these ideas and see how you can use them in your own practical work.

Creating meaning using explorative strategies

Imagine that you are given a photo and a newspaper article as stimuli. Your group might decide to create a still image based on the picture and add thought-tracking to indicate the feelings of the characters. You could develop the piece further by relating the picture to the article: a narrator recounts the story of the article while other members of the group adopt roles. The still image now becomes a photograph that appears with the article and at key points the characters step out of the image to reveal their thoughts or to enact events.

Olympic Dream!

Our town was made proud today when local girl, Jessica Davies, aged 21, came through the qualifying rounds to compete in the women's 100 metres at the Olympic Games later this year.

Jessica started running at her junior school at the tender age of ten. Progressing through to secondary, she was encouraged to train at a local running club by her sports teacher who spotted her potential. She then moved on to a professional running club aged seventeen.

Including the drama medium

○ *Lighting*: Sharply focused spotlights could light the still image and the narrator. This indicates the difference between the photo and the reported events.

○ *Space/levels*: The still image is raised on blocks and when characters step out to reveal their thoughts they move onto a lower level.

○ *Spoken language*: There is a difference between the language of the narrator and the more naturalistic language of the characters.

Selecting elements of drama

○ *Characterisation*: When individuals step out of the photograph, they become the characters from the newspaper article.

○ *Convention*: The still image is a frozen picture and the space is divided to indicate the newspaper and the real events in the story.

○ *Contrasts*: When the narrator is telling the story, there is stillness and a single voice. When the events are recreated, there is movement and maybe lots of voices.

What is important for success in Unit 1?

60

What is good practical work?

During your six-hour assessment you will be awarded marks for:

- how well you understand the dramatic potential of the theme, topic or issue

- how you respond to the use of strategies, elements and medium

- how committed and focused your involvement in practical work is

- how creative and imaginative your ideas are and how well you communicate them

- how you work with others to develop ideas.

Look at the diagram below. It shows a successful flow of initial ideas from the stimulus of a holiday brochure (also shown on page 93). It demonstrates how **explorative strategies**, **drama mediums** and the **elements of drama** can be developed.

(also shown on page 93)

edexcel examiner tip

- Respond imaginatively to the stimulus. The first idea you have might not be the most inspiring. Avoid the obvious and clichéd (what has become dull from overuse). Consider how you can examine the material in greater depth.

- Look for the dramatic potential in the stimulus. What opportunities does it provide? How can you use strategies, the drama mediums and elements to create a powerful piece of drama?

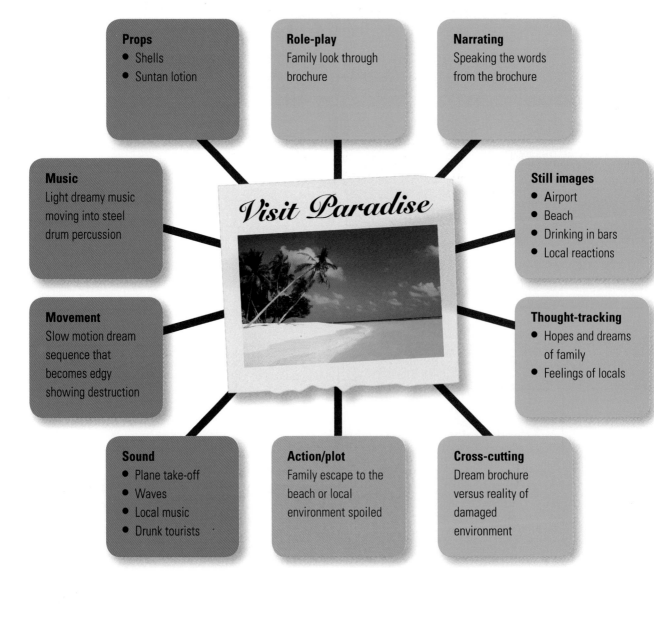

Props
- Shells
- Suntan lotion

Role-play
Family look through brochure

Narrating
Speaking the words from the brochure

Music
Light dreamy music moving into steel drum percussion

Visit Paradise

Still images
- Airport
- Beach
- Drinking in bars
- Local reactions

Movement
Slow motion dream sequence that becomes edgy showing destruction

Thought-tracking
- Hopes and dreams of family
- Feelings of locals

Sound
- Plane take-off
- Waves
- Local music
- Drunk tourists

Action/plot
Family escape to the beach or local environment spoiled

Cross-cutting
Dream brochure versus reality of damaged environment

What is a good documentary response?

In your documentary response, you will reflect on your own work and on the work of others. This part of the assessment enables you to show that you have understood the theme, topic or issue using the explorative strategies. Try to:

- evaluate the work rather than simply describing what you and the class did during the practical exploration
- reflect on how the drama medium, the elements of drama and the explorative strategies were used
- justify how and why you and your group chose the explorative strategies. Discuss how they deepened your understanding of meaning and of the topic, theme or issue
- comment on your personal journey during the practical exploration
- use the language of drama in your writing
- consider how you might present your documentary response: you can produce your work in visual as well as written form.

Your documentary response must be completed in controlled conditions but you will be able to refer to your notes.

Writing the documentary response is explored in detail later in this unit (see pages 97–99). Additionally, examples of documentary responses with examiner comments are included at the end of each practical exploration.

> **edexcel examiner tip**
>
> It is a good idea to keep a logbook of your practical explorations, so that you have reminders of what you did. This shouldn't be a diary or detailed record: don't write down everything you did. Note down key points and essential moments, using diagrams or annotated pictures where appropriate.

Sample Exploration 1: Outsiders

This exploration looks at the theme of 'outsiders', using different stimuli: film, photo, poetry and live theatre. Outsiders are individuals or groups of people who for some reason don't fit easily into society. People can be seen as outsiders for many different reasons, for example, because of their beliefs, appearance or abilities.

Stimuli: film and photograph

The first stimulus is the film, *The Elephant Man*, directed by David Lynch. Based on a true story, the film explores the life of John Merrick, a heavily disfigured Victorian man who was rescued from being displayed as a 'freak' in a circus by a surgeon, Frederick Treves, and then became a permanent resident at Whitechapel Hospital. Behind Merrick's outward appearance was a sensitive, intelligent person. The tag line of the film is 'I am not an animal! I am a human being!' The hood worn by Merrick was a 'mask' presenting a different 'face' to the public. In drama, masks convey an image to the spectator.

A still from the film The Elephant Man, *directed by David Lynch, released 1980, showing John Hurt as John Merrick.*

The cap and hood worn by the real John (Joseph) Merrick, now in the Royal London Hospital museum.

Using explorative strategies to respond to film stimuli

- Film is a visual medium, providing opportunities to create **still images** of key moments.

- **Narration**, used in a similar way to the convention of 'voiceover' in film, is an effective way of telling the story or commenting on the action.

- Film provides strong characters: you can explore their backgrounds and motives using **hot-seating**. You can also explore characters' feelings by **thought-tracking**.

Try it!

- Discuss the images on the opposite page. Why do you think people treated Merrick as a freak?
- Now use your body shape, facial expression and **levels** to create a **still image** of John Merrick. A documentary response to this is included on page 68.
- In one scene in the film, Merrick is taunted by a group of children who pull the hood from his head. In a group, create a **still image** of the scene and use the **convention** of **slow motion** to **mark the moment** when they pull the hood from his head. You could combine other strategies with the still image. For example, use **narration** to describe the scene or **thought-tracking** to reveal Merrick's feelings.
- You can develop this further by creating additional still images depicting key moments in Merrick's life, such as when he was exhibited as a freak and when he was rescued from the circus.

Relating the stimulus to wider issues

Nowadays we would not display people with physical deformities in a circus but some TV programmes do expose people with physical differences. This is often justified as 'helping' the people or 'educating' the general public.

Key terms
- **slow motion**
- **flashback**

Channel 4 screened a programme about a Chinese man afflicted with the same condition as John Merrick. It was called *The Elephant Man: Bodyshock Special* and provoked some passionate responses.

Discuss how you think John Merrick should be treated today. Consider the following questions:

- How do we respond to physical deformities in modern society?
- Is it right to intrude on the privacy of people who have physical differences?
- Would we pay to watch a freak show nowadays?

John 49
I am appalled that TV stations can broadcast the details of this grotesque condition. What about the privacy and dignity of the unfortunate individual?

Lucy 25
The trailer for this programme was deeply disturbing. It was screened at a time when my children were watching. What is to be gained from such programmes? I wonder whether the cynical broadcaster is simply seeking to increase viewer ratings. Our society seems obsessed with others' misfortunes.

Try it!

Use the strategies of role-play and cross-cutting to explore the issue of people's response to deformity.

- **Role-play** a scene where the nurses at Whitechapel Hospital discuss Merrick's deformities. They are afraid to touch him.
- **Cross-cut** into the role-play using the convention of **flashback** to show images playing in Merrick's memory, for example, the taunting of the children at the station and the reactions of the crowd at the freak show.

Now create a piece of drama that explores the responses to the *Bodyshock* documentary. For example, you could role-play an interview between a journalist and the documentary maker about the reasons for making this programme or role-play a telephone call from an outraged viewer to Ofcom complaining about the programme.

Stimuli: poem and artefact

In the 16th and 17th centuries it was common practice for people to be hunted down if there was a suspicion that they might be a witch. Witches were thought to have made a pact with the devil, giving them supernatural powers. In the poem below Beth Cross tells the story of a young girl accused of witchcraft.

Read the poem and look at the engraving of the famous 'witch-finder' Matthew Hopkins. The activities that follow explore the two different stimuli: a poem and an artefact. It is interesting to find links between the stimuli. Hopkins and witch-hunting are historical fact whereas the poem is fiction inspired by past events. In the poem the 'witch' is burned, whereas Hopkins' victims were hanged. Notice how Beth Cross explores the idea that men accused women of witchcraft as a means of revenge.

Background

- Matthew Hopkins was a notorious witch-finder responsible for more than 200 witches being hanged between 1645 and 1646.

- He was the son of a Puritan clergyman who believed that witches were at large and undermining 'godly' communities. More witches were hanged in Essex than in any other county.

- It was believed that accused women often had 'familiars' (pets who were the embodiment of the devil). Notice the animals in the woodcut.

- Some people took the opportunity to rid themselves of troublesome neighbours by dredging up family feuds and accusing each other of witchcraft.

- Strange goings-on in a village were investigated, from farm animals suddenly being taken sick to someone coming out in a rash! People were very quick to put the blame on an unpopular member of the community.

Witch Spawn

It's true I knew her Mother burned;
The girl seemed simple, free from guile;
Man is but man: my head was turned.
(A witch she was with her slow, rare smile.)

I have no knowledge of how she charmed,
Some said she fed on serpent's milk;
Yet child or beast she never harmed.
(A witch she was but her skin was silk.)

Small creatures answered to her call
Fearlessly running to her feet,
She lived amongst them: knew them all.
(A witch she was, so warm and sweet.)

Her eyes were neither blue nor grey,
So dark at night; I never did see
What colour they were by light of day.
(A witch she was as she lay with me.)

They say she bore the Devil's brat:
Only I and my mirror can tell
How often the Devil has worn my hat!
(A witch she was but she pleased me well.)

'She'll cast her eye on our men for sure,
And suck their wits!' the women said;
They stoned her windows and broke her door.
(A witch she was with her wild, dark head.)

They dragged her out to the market square
Half mad with fear, her hair close shorn;
The stake stood high and they bound her there.
(A witch she was, of a true witch born.)

She screamed and spat at the rush of flame
As it touched her flesh – and I half turned,
Fearing she might call my name …

A witch she was. As such – she burned.

Beth Cross

Black and white reproduction of a 17th-century wood engraving depicting the witch-finder Matthew Hopkins with two witches and their familiars.

Try it!

Discuss attitudes to witchcraft at this time. Why did people believe so strongly in witches? Now use a whole-class **role-play** to explore the issues. You should:

- imagine that you are the residents of a village gripped by the fear of witches
- each create your own role, for example, minister, midwife or farmer
- role-play a scene on the village green where people meet up. Rumours spread concerning a girl who is suspected of witchcraft.

Developing the drama

In groups, create a scene where a witch-finder is brought into the village.

- Roles: One person is the witch-finder and another becomes the accused girl. Others play villagers.
- Story: The girl is accused of causing the failure of the farmer's crops. She was seen making a doll by plaiting the corn.
- Action: Improvise the villagers' reactions to the witch-finder and to the accusation. Do they suspect the girl or could it be revenge for a family feud?
- The witch-finder asks the villagers questions.

Using forum theatre to explore viewpoints

Divide the villagers into two groups. The first group supports the witch-finder and suspects the girl; the second group does not want the witch-finder in its community and thinks that the girl is innocent.

- Play the scene where Hopkins takes the girl from her house and she protests her innocence.
- The spectators can stop the action at any point and give advice to an actor or take over a role.

Evaluating the response to this stimulus

Discuss the following questions in response to your work:

- How did the emotions in your drama response to the poem help you to create your character?
- Did the **role-play** work effectively? How was everyone involved?
- How was **spoken language** used to create roles and reflect the period?
- What did the **forum theatre** reveal about character and characters' relationships? (A documentary response to the forum theatre work is included on page 68.)
- What did you learn through the drama about how gossip and rumour can influence attitudes?

> **edexcel examiner tip**
> You will be assessed on how well you work in a group. So, when planning a group activity, make sure you listen carefully to others and respond to ideas positively.

Stimulus: live theatre production

The next stimulus linked to the theme of 'outsiders' is a piece of live theatre. Disability can make an individual feel like an outsider and sometimes disabled people feel that society does not acknowledge their needs. In *Flight Path*, by David Watson, Danny is a 25-year-old man with Down's Syndrome. The play traces the story of Danny's family and the strains put on relationships. Danny's father leaves, his mother needs to work and Jonathan, Danny's 18-year-old brother, feels pressured to take responsibility for Danny.

Read the following extract from the play. In this scene, Jonathan has returned from a night shift at the airport, where he works to support himself through his A-levels. His mother is at work and Danny needs looking after. Note that in the play script a 'beat' is a short pause.

Notice how the dialogue uses repetition and **ellipsis**. These techniques suggest that Danny is struggling to express his feelings.

Independent research

A play script can be a valuable stimulus for exploration of a theme or topic and visiting the theatre is an important aspect of your GCSE course. Live performances can be used as stimuli for Unit 1 in addition to the live performance you will analyse in Unit 2.

Key terms
- ellipsis

DANIEL: Mum said that we should go and see a film. (*Beat*)

JONATHAN: What?

DANIEL: (*producing a note*) And then we should go to Londis to get something for lunch, and then we should go and take me to the doctor's.

JONATHAN: It's eight o'clock in the morning.

DANIEL: Oh. Well what, well what are we going to do?

JONATHAN: Well what are we gonna do? (*Beat. He half laughs*) Danny I'm...I'm up all night at work, now I've gotta go to sleep, then I've gotta go to college (*Beat*) Y'know I've, I'm ... You know Dad's gone?

DANIEL: Yeah, Mum told me that (*Beat*) If I could see...if I could see...if I could see, where Dad was now...(*Beat*) I'd probably punch him. (*Beat*) And probably kill him. (*Beat*) Because of what he did to me. And what he did to Mum. And what he did to us.

(*Later in the scene*)

DANIEL: I, am, actually, a ...adult.(*Beat*) I just...I just wanna make my own decisions (*Beat*). That's all.

Danny (left) and Jonathan in a production of Flight Path.

David Watson, Flight Path

Discussing the extract

In your group discuss the following questions:

● How does Danny try to communicate his feelings?

● What is Jonathan's attitude to his brother?

● How does Danny feel about his father?

Try it!

In pairs, **role-play** the following scenes:

- Danny's conversation with his mother before she left for work
- Jonathan's discussion with his father about responsibility for Danny.

Then **hot-seat** Jonathan, Dad and Mum. Explore their relationships with Danny and how they feel about him.

> **(To Mum)** Is your career more important to you than looking after Danny?

> **(To Jonathan)** Do you feel resentful that you have to care for Danny?

> **(To Dad)** Did you leave because of the strain that Danny's care put on the family?

Explore the issues

This play raises some important issues about responsibility for disabled family members and society's attitudes to disability. We also see how Lauren, Jonathan's girlfriend, and Joe, his friend, respond to Danny. The play ends very positively with Jonathan and Lauren providing Danny with an allotment beneath the airport 'flight path'.

The plot of *Flight Path* reveals that, because Danny is 25 and an adult, he is no longer eligible for a residential school. He is unhappy at his adult independent living centre and, at the start of the play, returns to his family.

Try it!

Develop your exploration using forum theatre to consider attitudes and responsibilities to disability. Explore Danny's return to live with his family. Select one person to start off in each of the roles as below.

MOTHER

DANNY · **Forum theatre space** · FATHER

JONATHAN

Scene 1: Danny and Jonathan
DANNY: Who should look after me today?

Scene 2: Father and Mother
FATHER: You spend lots of time sorting out other people's problems because you're a social worker. Why don't you spend more time helping your own family?

Scene 3: Jonathan and Mother
JONATHAN: Do you expect me to look after Danny or work for my A-levels and open up opportunities for the future?

Scene 4: Danny and Father
DANNY: When you met a younger woman and left us, did you think about what would happen to me?

Now discuss what you have discovered about attitudes.

- Is Danny an outsider? If so, who is excluding him? How can he feel included and valued?
- Evaluate your use of **role-play**, **hot-seating** and **forum theatre**. How did they help you develop your exploration of outsiders?

Examples from documentary responses

Read the following examples of students' documentary responses on work related to the theme of outsiders and an examiner's comments on them. Think about how you can develop your own documentary responses on the work you have done.

This first extract describes a student's physical recreation of John Merrick's disabilities, in response to the film still on page 62.

edexcel examiner comment

This candidate has included precise detail and related the exercise to the meaning: that Merrick's deformity caused both emotional and physical discomfort. The candidate explains how he created the image using body shape and levels. He also reflects on his own emotional response.

> At the beginning of our lesson we had to look at a picture of John Merrick. We then had to base a freeze on John's body structure. When told to freeze I stood slightly crouched over with my back twisted to the side, my right arm was across my chest to resemble the deformities in his arm and my left arm was straight. Finally, my neck was leaning on my shoulder.
>
> Freezing is a good way of working because it helps the audience see all angles of the person freezing, which makes it clearer to the audience what the person is representing. Freezing can also put a lot more emphasis on a piece of drama. In this case it showed emphasis on John Merrick's deformities. This made me realise how difficult it was for John to do everyday things such as walking and getting out of bed.

The extract below is from a student's evaluation of the effectiveness of **forum theatre** to explore the topic of witch-hunting as on page 65.

edexcel examiner comment

Good examples of dialogue and some evaluative judgements.

> Another good moment during our forum theatre was when the accused witch was sent to the cells with other people inside there. Soon as she arrived they began asking questions such as 'why are you here?', 'did they accuse you too?'. The witch never replied, leaving a silence, which showed how awkward she was feeling. They then replied 'It's okay you can talk to us.'

edexcel examiner comment

A clear sense of how the space was used to create tension.

> It was a good use of space because when the other people were asking questions, the accused witch moved further and further away slowly. This showed she was feeling nervous and scared and that she didn't want to be a part of them.

edexcel examiner comment

The comment shows an awareness that forum theatre has not been used to its full potential. The response could be improved by including ideas on exactly how others might be involved and how this would have been helpful in the exploration.

> One thing that could have been improved was if more people joined in and other people came in and out of the forum theatre.

68

Sample Exploration 2: Tomorrow's World

This exploration looks at the future and uses a variety of different stimuli: a fiction story, a poem, a TV drama, a painting and music.

Stimulus: fiction

This first stimulus is a short story called *The Pedestrian* by Ray Bradbury. It is set in a future where 'The Machine' controls human beings. Leonard Mead rebels against the strict controls on his freedom by walking outside. The Machine forbids this and an unmanned police car arrests him. The message of this story is that our increasing dependence on machines could lead to a loss of freedom.

Read the extract below.

Sometimes he would walk for hours and miles and return only at midnight to his house. And on his way he would see the cottages and homes with their dark windows, and it was not unequal to walking through a graveyard ... Mr Leonard Mead would cock his head, listen, look, and march on... 'Hello, in there,' he whispered to every house on every side as he moved. 'What's up tonight on Channel 4, Channel 7, Channel 9?'... The street was silent and long and empty... 'What is it now?' he asked the houses, noticing his wrist watch. 'Eight-thirty pm? Time for a dozen assorted murders? A quiz? A revue? A comedian?'

Creating a **still image** would be an effective way of responding to this fiction extract, or similar fiction stimuli.

Key terms
• proxemics

Try it!

Create a **still image** representing Leonard Mead walking past the silent houses, in which people are watching television.

- Use different **levels**; not everyone in the house needs to be sitting.
- Consider the **proxemics**. (Check the definition of this term in the glossary at the back of this book.)
- Make sure that facial expression shows how the characters are feeling.
- How can you show that Leonard Mead is walking when the image is still?
- How can the image suggest that Mead's walking is unlawful and unusual?

Thought-tracking is a useful way of developing a still image and can be used to reveal the inner feelings of the characters in any fiction stimuli.

Try it!

Add **thought-tracking** to your **still image**. Consider the following:

- What are the people in the houses thinking? What are they thinking about the TV programmes? Have they noticed Leonard Mead? How might they respond?

- What might Leonard Mead be thinking? How does he feel about the people in the houses? He is breaking the law. Is he afraid? You could develop your thought-tracking into a **monologue** for Leonard.

Key terms
- monologue

The central part of the story describes Mead's arrest by the police. Read the extract below.

He was within a block of his destination when the lone car turned a corner quite suddenly and flashed a fierce white cone of light upon him... A metallic voice called to him:

'Stand still. Stay where you are! Don't move!'

He halted.

'Put up your hands!'

'But–' he said.

'Your hands up! Or we'll shoot!'

'Your name?' said the police car as if talking to itself. The light held him fixed, like a museum specimen, needle thrust through chest.

'Leonard Mead,' he said.

'Speak up!'

'What are you doing out?'

'Walking,' said Leonard Mead.

'Walking!'

'Just walking,' he said simply, but his face felt cold.

'Walking, just walking, walking?'

'Yes, sir.'

'Walking where? For what?'

'Walking for air. Walking to see.'

Try it!

Use **narration** and **role-play** to create the scene where the police car stops Mead.

- **Mark the moment** when he stops walking and realises that he has been caught.

- Consider how you might use **voice** and **spoken language** to suggest the 'metallic' voice of the car or to reflect Mead's emotions.

- Experiment with **lighting**, using a torch or flashlight to create the 'cone of light' that transfixes Mead.

Now evaluate the activity. Discuss the effectiveness of using these strategies and how they helped understanding of the issues the story explores.

Stimuli: poem and television

The next two stimuli for exploring the topic of the future are:

● a poem, 'If you push a button', by Japanese poet Takagi Kyozo

● a TV drama called *The Last Enemy*.

The poem and drama have similar messages: they warn how advances in technology could mean machines take over our activities and how surveillance could be used to control every aspect of our lives.

Read the poem, noticing how the poet shrinks the human action (of pushing a button) as the poem progresses.

You might be able to find extracts from the drama *The Last Enemy* on the internet. The drama begins when Stephen Ezard, the main character, receives news of his brother's death and so returns to Britain after a long time away. He finds that the UK is a very different place from when he left, where terrorism and illegal immigration are commonplace and TIA (Total Information Awareness) has been introduced. This centralised database of information means that each citizen's every move can be tracked and monitored quickly and easily, and as Stephen tries to uncover the real reasons for his brother's death his efforts are frustrated at every turn. He find himself unable to access public transport, his place of work, or even his bank account, and a normal life becomes impossible.

The producer of *The Last Enemy*, Gub Neal, described the programme as 'a cautionary tale about technology, with identity cards, biometric tests and armed police becoming an everyday presence in our lives. It's predictive, rather than science fiction, because CCTV cameras and loyalty cards mean we are already being monitored.'

If you push a button

If you push a button
a door opens

you push a button
it is light even at night

push button
You make a non-stop trip to the 100th floor

push button
You hear music

p button
The world news becomes available

button
Our activities are photographed and our
 words recorded

but
The police are called out

bu
A patrol car appears

b
We vanish

Takagi Kyozo
translated by James Kirkup

Try it!

In your group, use the drama forms **physical theatre** and **sound** to explore the poem. For example, physically create the lift and add appropriate sounds.

Now **role-play** a scene from *The Last Enemy* using your own language. Add a narration for Stephen Ezard showing his thoughts.

Now use **mime**, physical theatre and sound to create a piece of drama that explores how an innocent person is rendered powerless by surveillance technology. Try to show the gradual process, as the poem does, through your language.

edexcel examiner tip

Using explorative strategies effectively

When you're responding to a stimulus, try to avoid simply copying it in your drama work, for example, reading out the words of a poem or acting out a scene from a TV series in a naturalistic style. Instead, aim to be creative with the poet's language and the themes of the episode. Use the stimuli as a springboard for your own creative ideas.

Key terms
• physical theatre

Stimuli: a painting and music

The final two stimuli in this sample exploration are:

- *The Persistence of Memory* by Salvador Dalí, a surrealist painting of clocks that appear to be melting
- the Pink Floyd song 'Time', which begins with an echo of ticking clocks and builds up to a climax of bells and alarm clocks all sounding at once.

The Persistence of Memory *by Salvador Dalí*

Try it!

Think about the meaning of the two stimuli.

- What might be happening in the song?
- What might be implied by clocks ringing and chiming in this jarring way?
- What does the picture make you think about?
- What do you think the artist was trying to express through this work?

How to respond effectively to music and art as stimuli

- Consider the key themes and explore what the artist or composer was trying to say to the audience.
- Think about the dramatic elements of the sound, the colour, the light and the composition.
- Brainstorm the ideas stimulated by listening to the music and looking at the painting.

Try it!

Working in a group with one person acting as a sculptor, create a still image of a sculpure for an art gallery with the title *Tomorrow's World*.

- The image should have levels and fine detail.
- The work should be symbolic, not naturalistic.
- The message should be clear.

Then evaluate the image and discuss how you engaged with the theme and drew on the stimuli.

Try it!

Working in a group, create a non-naturalistic piece of drama in the style of the painting and music.

Firstly, create a spider diagram that records all your responses to the music and painting. These can be related to the message of the stimuli or they might suggest dramatic ideas using light, sound or props. Look at the example below.

Now decide on the form that your drama piece will take.

● Will there be a story?

● Will you use spoken language or **total theatre** with mime, music, masks and lighting?

● How will you create the climax of the piece theatrically?

Below is one group's initial ideas in response to the two stimuli.

Key terms
● total theatre

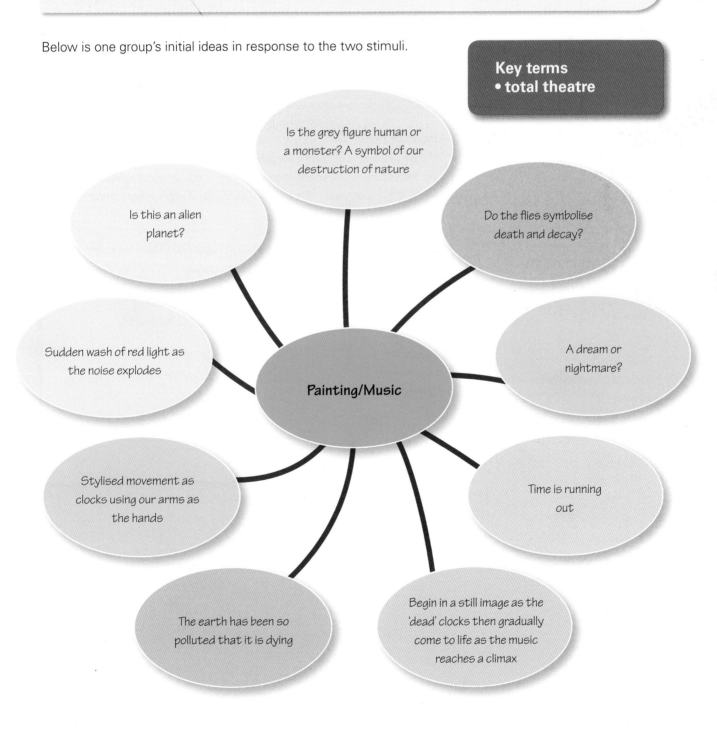

Is the grey figure human or a monster? A symbol of our destruction of nature

Is this an alien planet?

Do the flies symbolise death and decay?

Sudden wash of red light as the noise explodes

Painting/Music

A dream or nightmare?

Stylised movement as clocks using our arms as the hands

Time is running out

The earth has been so polluted that it is dying

Begin in a still image as the 'dead' clocks then gradually come to life as the music reaches a climax

The notes below are from a group that created a piece of drama in response to these two stimuli. The piece was called *Poisoned Earth*. The notes have been annotated to show you how they link to the group's initial ideas and to the requirements of the documentary response.

Key terms
• **backstory**
• **dialogue**

Meaning and message.

> **Narrative**: Earth has become uninhabitable because of pollution. Humans must start life on a new planet.

> **Form**: One character tells the story through monologue. Movement, slow motion and gesture convey the action. No spoken **dialogue**.

The monologue picks up this theme from the initial ideas.

> **From monologue**: Earth is dead. Polluted, barren, without hope. We did not listen to the warnings, we continued to drive our cars, fly our planes and cover our green fields with houses. Here, a new planet….it is cold, colder than the Earth…strange noises…time…time has run out….

Use of explorative strategies – still image and narration.

> **Use of stimulus**: Opens with still image, students are the melted clocks and the grey figure is the human being. Music begins; he/she rises and narrates the **backstory** over the quiet section of the track. On the discordant bells the 'clocks' slowly rise and move in a synchronised way towards the central figure.

> **Use of vocal sound**: Each 'clock' creates a unique sound as a 'language'. This is repeated as the central character is surrounded.

Use of the drama medium.

> **Use of light**: The studio is lit in blue to create a cold, harsh atmosphere. At the climax of sound, the lights begin a slow cross-fade to red.

Note the use of contrast between silence and high volume.

> **Climax**: The human is engulfed by the advancing 'clocks' which then return to their former positions. The human lies as the grey figure in the foreground. The music fades out.

Example from a documentary response

Here is an extract from a student's documentary response to their group's practical exploration on The Future, using the stimuli of the poem 'If you push a button' and the TV drama *The Last Enemy*. The examiner's comments are included as annotations.

As you read, think about how you can develop your own documentary response on the work you have done.

We began by creating a soundscape of machine sounds… This was effective because it created a world of inhuman machines. The studio was totally dark and this heightened the atmosphere.

The group entered the space, each one under a sharp spotlight and physically became the machines from the poem: a lift, a microwave, a bank cash point. I played Stephen Ezard and my challenge was that there was no dialogue so I had to convey my emotions through facial expression and movement. This provided a unique opportunity to focus on non-verbal skills. I moved cautiously, pausing to look anxiously over my shoulder.

The 'news' on a laptop (played by another student) was spoken in a harsh mechanical voice: it told me that I was a 'non-person' and that the authorities were searching for me. The vocal tone was menacing and created an alarming mood: I reacted by showing the shock on my face. I rushed from one machine to another becoming more frantic as each machine rejected me with abrasive mechanised voices e.g. 'Rejected! Non person! Security alert!'

This climax was very effective as it showed how easily a human being can be dominated by machines. The addition of blue light created a cold atmosphere. At the end the machines advanced towards me robotically repeating their phrases. The final moment came when I collapsed onto the floor shielding my eyes; we added a single harsh spotlight. When I looked up all the machines had gone. My final expression was of bewildered resignation.

This work really made me question how far machines have become a threat to our freedom rather than an aid to our comfort.

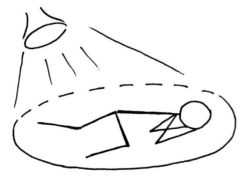

edexcel examiner comment

The description is detailed.

edexcel examiner comment

The candidate describes the response to the challenge of having to convey emotion without words.

edexcel examiner comment

Notice the precise description of vocal tone.

edexcel examiner comment

The candidate carefully evaluates the effectiveness of each aspect of the drama.

edexcel examiner comment

The candidate shows an understanding of the use of lighting as a symbol.

edexcel examiner comment

There is some understanding of the issues and how the exploration created meaning, but the candidate could have added an example of how machines are impacting on 21st-century life, linking this to their practical work.

Sample Exploration 3: Stolen Lives

This exploration looks at the topic of stolen lives (the loss of millions of men during the First World War) using stimuli such as posters, photographs, newspaper articles, poems, letters and play scripts.

Stimuli: poster, photograph and newspaper article

The first group of stimuli are about the recruitment of soldiers. Look at the poster, photograph and newspaper article below.

Our Country Needs Us!

Last night, three hundred people crammed into a dark, cheerless village hall in a small village in Staffordshire. Before the meeting was over, thirty-five men had walked out and enlisted. At the end of the meeting someone called 'Three cheers for the King!' and a woman stood up and cried, 'Three cheers for our recruits!' I don't believe there was an eligible man in that audience who didn't end up offering his services.

Using explorative strategies to respond to the stimuli

Still images and **thought-tracking** are effective ways of exploring these stimuli. These strategies enable you to create a sequence of images to tell the story while also focusing on the emotions of the characters. They can be used effectively for any type of stimulus that builds up an image in your mind or introduces you to people in specific situations.

Try it!

Create a series of **still images** showing the following:

- Young men responding enthusiastically at a village hall meeting
- Men queuing at a recruiting office to join up
- Women waving the men off to war.

Present your images one after the other, moving smoothly between them to create snapshots of a story.

Add **thought-tracking** to your still images. Think carefully about how people appear to feel and what their innermost thoughts might be. They could be very different! For example, a mother cheerfully waving her son goodbye might actually feel extremely worried and upset.

Remember the qualities of a good still image: levels, facial expression, stillness, energy and meaning.

Refer to pages 81 and 82 for an example of a documentary response recording this task.

Stimulus: poem

The next stimulus is a poem, *The Send Off*, by Wilfred Owen, which describes the new recruits going away to war. Notice how at first they appear happy (the word 'gay' in this context means light-hearted) but there is a haunting suggestion throughout the poem that they may not return.

The Send Off

Down the close, darkening lanes they sang their way
To the siding-shed,
And lined the train with faces grimly gay.

Their breasts were stuck all white with wreath and spray
As men's are, dead.

Dull porters watched them, and a casual tramp
Stood staring hard,
Sorry to miss them from the upland camp.
Then, unmoved, signals nodded, and a lamp
Winked to the guard.

So secretly, like wrongs hushed-up, they went.
They were not ours:
We never heard to which front these were sent.

Nor there if they yet mock what women meant
Who gave them flowers.

Shall they return to beatings of great bells
In wild trainloads?
A few, a few, too few for drums and yells,
May creep back, silent, to still village wells
Up half-known roads.

Wilfred Owen

Using hot-seating to explore a stimulus

Hot-seating helps to develop your understanding of character. Make sure that questions explore the character in depth. For example:

- To a mother, 'Did you try to persuade your son not to join up?'
- To a volunteer, 'Have you joined up because war sounds exciting or are you driven by your desire to fight for your country?'

Try it!

Bearing in mind the poem, **hot-seat** these characters:

- A mother, wife or girlfriend who has given flowers to her departing hero
- A soldier waiting for the train
- A porter at the station
- A tramp who watches the soldiers leave for war.

Then **role-play** a scene which explores one of these scenarios.

Stimulus: play script

The next stimulus comes from Joan Littlewood's play, *Oh What a Lovely War*. She used **back projection** of war photographs, songs and humour to make a serious point about the futility of war.

In one of scenes, volunteers are trained to use a rifle by 'Sergeant Major', who is represented as a comic character. The recruits are inept and the humour is both physical and verbal.

> ## Key terms
> • **back projection**

The Sergeant Major begins by calling the new recruits a 'lousy lot' and telling them he's going to teach them how to fix a bayonet to their rifles. He then shoots a quickfire series of orders at the recruits, telling them exactly how they should handle their rifle to get it into position: '...on your left shoulder, left hand parallel to the ground, right hand down...' Some of the recruits struggle to keep up with the Sergeant Major's orders or follow his movements and he picks on the worst performing volunteer by telling him 'I'll have your bloody guts for garters in a minute'. The Sergeant Major then demonstrates how to fix the bayonet and bellows his instructions at the recruits, counting them out so that they follow his example: 'one - two - three - Fix.' When he spots that one of the recruits cannot find his bayonet, the Sergeant Major walks up to him and says 'Hello, hello, hello, hello. Where's your bayonet?' The difficulty the recruits have in following the Sergeant Major's quickfire demonstration and his reaction to them is a real source of humour in the scene, but also suggests how the recruits are not ready or well prepared to go to war.

One of the best ways to use a play script stimulus is to enact one of the existing scenes, drawing out your own interpretation.

Try it!

Role-play the scene, with one person taking on the role of the Sergeant Major, and the rest of the group as recruits.

- Use short sticks or other **props** as rifles.
- Work on the humour of the scene: the comedy lies in the inability of the recruits to handle the rifles and in their reactions to the Sergeant.
- If you are the Sergeant, think about speaking some sections of the speech to individuals. How might they react?

During this activity think carefully how you use the drama media of **space**, **movement**, **voice**, **spoken language** and the elements of drama such as **characterisation** and **pace**.

Stimuli: letter and poem

The next two stimuli give evidence of the conditions the soldiers endured at the front.

My Dearest Mother
We had practically nothing to do for the first two days then ... we noticed volumes of dense yellow smoke rising up and coming towards the British Trenches...it makes your eyes smart and run, I became violently sick...By this time the din was something awful... we had to lie flat in the trenches. This went on all night and all next day...We could not get rations up to us and what with hunger and cold it was awful. One poor beggar came along crying for someone to tie his arm up...the arm was completely off up to the elbow, a fearful sight.

From a letter written by Lance Corporal Jim Keddie, 4 May 1915.

Breakfast

We ate our breakfast lying on our backs
Because the shells were screeching overhead
I bet a rasher to a loaf of bread
That Hull United would beat Halifax
When Jimmy Stainthorpe played full-back instead
Of Billy Bradford. Ginger raised his head
And cursed, and took the bet, and dropt back dead,
We ate our breakfast lying on our backs
Because the shells were screeching overhead

Wilfred Gibson

Stimuli that describe a historical setting and events can be explored using **role-play** and **movement**. The poem suggests dialogue whereas the letter describes action, but you could combine the two elements using a **narrator** to give a commentary. Narrating can communicate violent action or re-tell complicated events. Shakespeare used this device to tell the audience about battles which took place off stage.

Try it!

Create a short drama using the roles suggested by the stimuli.

Consider the **spoken language** and **voices**. Where do you think the soldiers are from? Can you use an appropriate accent?

How can **movement** be used to create the physical action? You might use the **convention** of slow motion.

Creating contrasts

Contrast can be a powerful element of drama. Stimuli can be explored and developed to create contrasts which give a powerful message.

When the soldiers marched away to war, they were proud and excited at the prospect of fighting for their country. The families at home were often protected from the truth: many men wrote cheerful letters and the government kept up the spirits of the people at home by giving them good news about victory while concealing the death count.

Try it!

Imagine the following scenario and create a short drama to convey it: a group of soldiers are in a trench writing the truth in their diaries but sending home cheerful, positive letters.

You could use **cross-cutting** to go from women reading letters aloud, to the trenches, where men are writing their diaries. Speak the words that they write aloud.

Below is an example of some students' work on this activity.

MOTHER:
(reading Jim's letter)

My dear mother, I am doing well here. The food is not too bad and we sometimes have bacon for breakfast – it reminds me of the morning smell in our kitchen. Yesterday we were attacked in the trench by gas but I only had sore eyes. Got off lightly.

JIM: (writing his diary) Gas attack! Vile yellow mist that destroys the lungs. Yesterday a good friend died horribly. He could not breathe, he passed out and drowned in the mud before anyone noticed. Today we ate a ration of charred bacon, lying on our backs as the shells whistled over us. I bet Ginger that Hull would beat Halifax – he jumped up suddenly – caught a bullet and died. When will this hell end?

Exploring the issue

You could develop this activity by creating a scene that **cross-cuts** from a modern war zone, where soldiers are experiencing appalling dangers, to their families at home. Instead of letters being written and read you could use emails, newspaper articles or TV reports.

Discuss the similarities and differences between the experiences of soldiers and their families in World War One and today. For example, modern television coverage means that families at home can see some of the realities of war but, even today, some details are kept secret for security reasons.

Example from a documentary response

Here is an extract from a student's documentary response to their group's practical exploration on stolen lives, using the stimuli of the newspaper article, a recruitment poster and a photograph of a recruitment office. The student explains how the group used the explorative strategies of **still imaging** and **thought-tracking**. The examiner's comments are included alongside the work. As you read, think about how you can develop your own documentary response to the work you have done.

Still image 1: The village hall

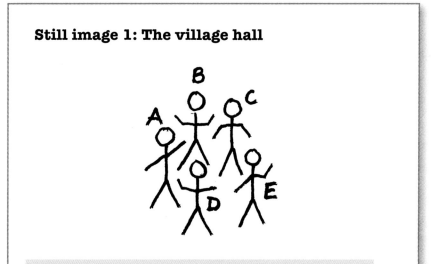

- We stood very close to suggest that we were in a crowd.

- Strained our necks to create the idea that we were looking over others' heads to the stage.

- Energy in the image to show our enthusiasm.

- Hands in the air recreating our cheering the speaker.

We spoke our thoughts using thought-tracking:

A = My children will be proud of me.

B = I will come back a hero and my girlfriend will be so proud.

C = I can feel the excitement in the room.

D = I am terrified, I don't want to die but I don't want to be a coward.

E = If I pretend to be older I can join up.

We moved using the convention slow motion into the next image. We added the drama medium of music by singing 'Pack up your troubles' very slowly as we moved. This created a sombre atmosphere that had a sense of foreboding.

> **edexcel examiner comment**
> The bulleted points give a very clear indication of how the still image was created and links the decisions to the issues raised in the stimuli.

> **edexcel examiner comment**
> The music/singing (drama medium) and the convention slow motion are clearly employed to create meaning and develop the exploration of the issue.

Still image 2: The recruiting office

- There was less energy in this image, to show that a sense of reality was dawning.
- Hands were now down, by our sides or in pockets.
- The image showed that doubts were creeping into our minds.

Thought-tracking:

A = I hope to live to see my son's first birthday.

B = I know it's right to fight for your country.

C = There are so many men joining up – I can't turn away now.

D = What if my girlfriend finds someone else while I am away?

E = I'll tell them I'm 18 then I can go to war!

edexcel ▦ examiner comment

The spoken language in the thought-tracking shows a perceptive understanding of emotions.

We then moved in slow motion to a final image. This time we sang 'It's a long way to Tipperary' slowly as we moved.

Still image 3: Women of Britain say go!

- The hand up waving mirrors the men in the village hall.
- The image had less energy, as if the women had some fears.
- Levels were used to create the different ages:

        mother standing

        grandmother seated

        child straining on toes to look out of the window

edexcel ▦ examiner comment

Precise detail included with references to the meaning created.

edexcel ▦ examiner comment

The student explains how levels were used to create the image.

Thought-tracking:

A = Come back, please come back, I'll wait for you.

B = My only son, going to war. He will be a hero.

C = Bye bye Daddy.

Sample Exploration 4: Stand Up for Your Rights!

This exploration looks at the topic of protest and uses a variety of different stimuli such as newspaper headlines, a diary extract, a photograph and a poem. This section focuses on two protests:

- The suffragette protest at women's lack of a right to vote in the early 20th century

- The student protest in Tiananmen Square, Bejing, in 1989, against the lack of democratic rights in China.

Stimulus: newspaper headlines

Women were not given the right to vote in parliamentary elections until after World War 1. Before then, many women campaigned for 'suffrage' (the right to vote) and they became known as suffragettes. Their campaign began peacefully, but became increasingly violent. Newspapers reported the suffragettes' campaign closely. Read the headlines below.

SUFFRAGETTE WOMEN BREAK WINDOWS IN OXFORD STREET

WOMEN GO ON HUNGER STRIKE IN PRISON

WOMEN CHAIN THEMSELVES TO RAILINGS AT BUCKINGHAM PALACE

BLACK FRIDAY! WOMEN INJURED IN VIOLENT PROTEST

DEEDS NOT WORDS! VIOLENCE ON THE LONDON STREETS

KING'S HORSE KILLS EMILY DAVISON AT DERBY

Newspapers, and their headlines in particular, can be effective stimuli because they summarise events very tightly and often have a dramatic content. Headlines can be the stimulus to explore events in greater detail, or they can be incorporated into a mini drama of their own.

> **Key terms**
> - montage

Try it!

Use the headlines above to create a **montage** of the events reported, by **role-playing** newspaper sellers on a busy street, calling out the different headlines to passers by. Vendors can compete for custom by trying to out-shout each other, or by making their headlines sound the most dramatic.

The headline describing the death of Emily Davison is the most shocking. Use a strategy to **mark the moment** when this is announced. Think carefully about how to make this as effective as you can.

- All other vendors could stop and turn to face the one with this headline.
- The vendor with this headline stands on a block. The rest all freeze.
- An audible gasp from all news vendors following this headline.

Stimulus: diary

The next stimulus is an extract based on a diary written by Mary, a suffragette in prison. She describes how she was force-fed during a hunger-strike protest.

I heard knocking on the walls, and all the prisoners were shouting that they had not eaten their food. Neither had I. The cell door opened and a doctor and three wardresses came in. One of the women asked me why I had not eaten my food. I refused to speak. She said, 'Food has been brought for you. This is your last chance to eat of your own free will'. Still I did not answer. 'Well, I have no other course than to compel you!' she barked.

The wardresses held me down and the doctor pushed a tube into my nostrils; there was a terrible pain in my ears and chest. He stood on a chair, holding the funnel end of the tube above my head. He poured a mixture of egg and milk into the funnel. When they had finished they left, without a word, and went to force-feed someone else.

A diary is useful stimulus because it gives an insight into feelings as well as events. Various explorative strategies can be used to develop this sort of stimulus into drama ideas.

Background information

- Many suffragettes were arrested and imprisoned.

- In 1909, Marion Dunlop started a hunger strike. Other imprisoned suffragettes adopted this form of protest.

- The authorities, afraid that the death of a suffragette would increase public sympathy, force-fed the strikers.

- In 1913, after a public outcry at the indignity of this practice, the government passed the Cat and Mouse Act. Striking prisoners were released and re-arrested when they had eaten enough to recover!

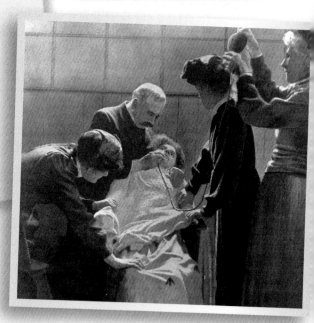

A suffragette being force-fed in prison.

Try it!

Role-play the scene of a suffragette being force-fed in prison. Use Mary as a **narrator** to comment on the story. You could use the convention of dividing the stage in two: one part showing the discussion between the doctor and wardress; the other showing the prison cell.

Consider the **rhythm** and **tempo** of the scene. Decide which sections should be played slowly and which fast. Think about the use of freeze frames and slow motion.

Exploring controversy

The suffragettes' protests were very controversial. Some people were against women having the vote; others supported their aims but not their methods of protest. Many suffragettes were married. Imagine how Mary's husband might have felt when she was released from prison, in order to eat again. Do you think his feelings would be of relief or concern, or both?

Role-play and forum theatre are two effective strategies for exploring controversial issues because they can focus on more than one viewpoint.

Try it!

In pairs, role-play one of these scenes:

- Mary meets a fellow suffragette to discuss the next act of protest.
- Mary's husband discusses his fears for her safety with a friend.

With your partner evaluate what the role-play revealed about the feelings aroused by how suffragettes were treated.

Use a forum theatre activity to examine both sides of the argument. You will work in two groups: one represents Mary and the other, her husband. One person from each group should take on the role of Mary or her husband.

Act out the argument: Mary intends to break the law again, but her husband tries to dissuade her. The rest of the group can intervene, calling 'Stop!' and either give advice to the character or take over the role.

After each side has called three 'stops', finish the scene and discuss the arguments presented. Who was the most powerful? Why? How was language used persuasively?

Independent research

Do some further research about the suffragettes' protests. In particular, find out about Black Friday, 1910, when hundreds of women were arrested, and the window-smashing campaign in Oxford Street in 1912.

While you carry out your research, think carefully about how you can explore your findings creatively using the drama strategies. For example, you could use:

- slow motion to portray the violent clash with the police
- thought-tracking of newspaper reporters at the scene
- a monologue in which a woman reflects on her experiences.

Stimulus: photograph

This iconic image of the lone protester came to symbolise the injustice of events in Tiananmen Square, where protesters were brutally suppressed by the Chinese army. Videos of this event, including Kate Adie's BBC news coverage, are available on YouTube.

A lone protestor faces Chinese tanks in Tiananmen Square in 1989.

Using photographs as stimuli

When using photographs as stimuli it is often helpful to approach them with a series of questions. For example:

- What is dramatic in this picture?
- Who might have taken this photo and why?
- Is the setting one of conflict or harmony, or are there contrasts within it?
- What is the overall mood? For example, tension, relaxation, fun, excitement, fear, sadness or tragedy.

Background information

- The Tiananmen Square protests of 1989 culminated in the Tiananmen Square Massacre (referred to in China as the 'June Fourth Incident').
- Protesters, mainly students, occupied Peking's (now known as Bejing) huge square and took part in a peaceful protest demanding freedom and democracy.
- The violent military attack on the protesters by Chinese government troops left hundreds dead or injured.
- China banned the foreign press from the country and strictly controlled coverage of the events.
- The violent suppression of the Tiananmen Square protest received widespread international condemnation.

Try it!

Look carefully at the photograph of the Tiananmen Square protester. With a partner, consider the drama and tension in the picture, and explore it further using the following strategies:

- Create a **still image** of protesters. Build this gradually using **walk-in freeze frame**. Do not shape and position your still image but walk into the space one at a time. Be aware of others' **shapes** and **levels**. Make sure that you add to the picture in an interesting way.
- **Mark the moment** when the lone protester confronts the tank.
- Use **monologue** or **narration** in role as news reporters to describe and comment on events as they unfold.
- **Hot-seat** the lone protester to discover his thoughts and fears.
- Use **fragmented monologue** to explore the thoughts and feelings of different characters in the scene, for example, the reporter, the tank driver or the lone protester.

Stimulus: poem

The poem *Tiananmen* was written by James Fenton, a British journalist
in China, ten days after the 4 June massacre in Tiananmen Square.
Fenton's poem was originally published in a newspaper.

Tiananmen

Tiananmen is broad and clean
And you can't tell where the dead have been
And you can't tell what happened there
And you can't speak of Tiananmen

You cannot speak, you cannot think
You dip your brush in ink
You cannot say what happened then
What happened then in Tiananmen

The cruel men are old and deaf
Ready to kill but short of breath
And they will die like other men
And lie in state in Tiananmen

They lie in state they lie in style
And other lives thrown on a pile
Thrown on a pile by cruel men
To cleanse the blood of Tiananmen

Truth is a secret keep it dark
Keep it dark in your heart of hearts
Keep it dark till you know when
The truth may return to Tiananmen

Tiananmen is broad and clean
And you can't tell where the dead have been
And you can't say when they'll come again
Come again to Tiananmen

James Fenton

When using poetry as a stimulus, think carefully about how the poet
is using language, as well as what he or she is saying. The language
of poetry relies on patterns, which can be used to dramatic effect.
Repetition of verses, sounds, words, rhyme and rhythm can be
explored in a dramatic performance with great effect.

Try it!

As a group, experiment with different ways of presenting the poem. Think carefully about using
spoken language and choreographed movement. Also consider how you can use climax and
anti-climax effectively. Here are some ideas:

- Use some verses as a chorus.
- Single voices echoing from different directions could create a sense of secrecy.
- Add light or music to increase the atmosphere.
- Look for clues as to the sort of voice to use. For example, 'Truth is a secret keep it dark' suggests a
  whisper.

Reflecting on the issues

The suffragettes and the Tiananmen protesters wanted the right to
have a political voice that gave them a say in how their country was
governed. How did your work in drama bring out this point? Which
strategies were effective in creating meaning?

Discuss how your work has deepened your understanding of the
reasons why people protest.

Example from a documentary response

Here is an extract from a student's documentary response to their group's practical exploration on protest, using the stimuli of the newspaper headlines about the suffragettes and one prisoner's diary. The student explains how the group produced a 'role on the wall' for Mary, in preparation for dramatising the force-feeding scene.

The examiner's comments are included alongside the work. As you read, think about how you can develop your own documentary response on the work you have done.

When our group worked on the force-feeding scene I played Mary. The role on the wall shows:

- how I felt
- how I wanted to be seen by others
- how others saw me.

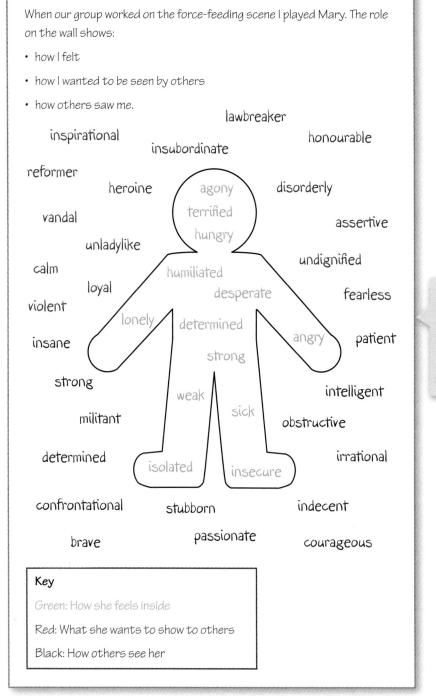

Key

Green: How she feels inside

Red: What she wants to show to others

Black: How others see her

edexcel ▦ examiner comment

The role on the wall shows the student's insight into the characterisation and emotions of Mary.

The aspects of the drama medium that we used were voice and movement, space, levels and lighting. We also included the drama elements of climax, characterisation and convention.

The drama began with a still image of Mary before the doctor and wardresses came into the cell. I spoke aloud as narrator; this strategy enabled me to tell the story and to reveal my emotions. As I have indicated on the 'role on the wall', I felt terrified yet strong and although I was hungry I was determined to be brave and to be loyal to the cause. Our exploration of the issue made me realise that the doctor, who was male, and even the wardresses, who were female, felt that I was a militant lawbreaker who was behaving in an undignified way. Many thought that enduring force-feeding was insane and thought that the women should go meekly back to their husbands.

When the feeding began, we froze the action at key points to enable me to narrate the events and my feelings. As the tube was inserted into my nose, I described the sickness and agony and reflected on the doctor's opinion of me: stubborn, irrational woman. In role, I recalled the reasons for the protest and remembered the other women for whom I was suffering. Although humiliated by the process I did not lose my passion. My facial expression and vocal tone reflected my fear and my courage.

The lighting was a hard edged, cold spotlight with a pale blue gel. This effectively created the atmosphere of the prison cell. We mimed the tubing but the detail of the movements of the doctor and my reactions made the scene very convincing.

edexcel examiner comment
There is a strong awareness of the uses of the drama medium.

edexcel examiner comment
The student shows she has understood how the process of creating the 'role on the wall' has informed her characterisation.

edexcel examiner comment
She has reflected on the meanings created in the drama and demonstrated an appreciation of the issues.

Sample Exploration 5: Fragile Earth

90

This exploration looks at the environment. In particular, it focuses on our responsibility for safeguarding the natural world and the different cultures that depend on it.

Stimulus: newspaper article

The newspaper article below recounts the sighting of a tribe, known as the Yanomami, in the Amazon rainforest. Read the article and discuss what the tribesmen might think about the plane and what the passengers on the plane might think about the tribesmen.

SURVIVAL OF A LOST RAINFOREST TRIBE

by Tim Spanton

The frantic and frightened painted faces of a lost tribe stare up as they raise simple weapons to ward off a beast from the skies.

The intruder – an aeroplane – had interrupted their daily lives deep in Brazil's Amazon rainforest.

The pictures astonished millions of people around the world yesterday. For they provided proof that, almost unbelievably, a hidden society had survived into the 21st century – untainted by the good or the bad of Western civilisation.

Although there was little information about them, tribal affairs experts said they resembled the well-studied Yanomami, who live a few miles north.

Background information

- The Yanomami culture has remained largely unchanged since the Stone Age.
- They gather fruit and hunt animals in their local environment.
- Before 1950 they had no contact with the outside world. Since then, westerners have brought disease and forest clearance is destroying their habitat.

Try it!

Create a **still image** depicting the moment when the Yanomami see the plane. Add **thought-tracking** to the still image of the Yanomami to reveal their emotions and fears.

Cross-cut to a **role-play** of the conversation in the plane when the passengers see the tribe. Contrast the thoughts of the Yanomami with the thoughts of the people in the plane. Think about the differences in **spoken language**.

Newspaper articles are effective stimuli because they sum up a situation or event in few words but with maximum impact. Many explorative strategies can be used with such stimuli including **role-play**, **still images** and **thought-tracking**. It is often useful to find out more information about the topic in the article.

Stimulus: artefacts

The next stimuli are artefacts. These can be works of art, pictures, historical or everyday objects. Looking at artefacts can provide a fascinating stimulus for explorative drama. You can focus on different aspects:

- where they are from (place and time)
- who used/ate/wore/made them
- how they were made
- why they were made.

Look carefully at the artefacts below. Brainstorm associations with each item.

Independent research

Think about the effects of western consumerism on the native people of the Amazon rainforest. You could research some of the following points and think about how you might communicate your thoughts on this topic in your drama work.

- How the Amazon rainforest is being cleared by logging to supply wood to make furniture for western markets
- How forest land is being destroyed to graze beef cattle for the western meat market
- How gold miners take valuable minerals from the land but bring diseases to local tribes who have no immunity.

Try it!

Use the ideas triggered by the artefacts as starting points for your drama. Use cross-cutting to draw out contrasts.

- Role-play some western students buying a beef burger after a night out. Cross-cut to the Yanomami struggling to survive.
- Role-play choosing a gold necklace to wear at a party. Cross-cut to the sickness brought by the miners to the tribe.
- You might want to work with a series of still images or with mime, linked by narration.

Making connections

In drama, you can connect ideas and create meaning using a technique called **juxtaposition**. This involves presenting two scenes or images one after the other and allowing the audience to make the connections. Similarities and contrasts can be highlighted.

> **Key terms**
> • juxtaposition
> • gobo
> • gels

Try it!

Development using the drama medium

Use the drama medium to develop your drama from page 91 and use juxtaposition to draw out meaning. You should use lighting to bring out the contrasts between the scenes. For example use harsh, stark shop lighting for the fast food outlet, but contrast this with a **gobo** and green **gels** to indicate the rainforest canopy in the Yanomami setting.

Use music to create mood and atmosphere. Play a modern track, possibly indicating a radio, in the western scenes. Contrast this with sounds of the rainforest or tribal music played on wind instruments.

Develop this scene using props. The Western explorers might carry cameras or specialised equipment. The Yanomami have bows and arrows or spears. Are there any simple items of set that you could use to suggest the two different settings?

Think carefully how to communicate contrasts between the two communities and lifestyles through costume. How can you represent one community living in a warm climate, leading physically active lives, and another community living in a cooler climate, using clothes and jewellery to display wealth and fashion trends?

Consider how you might use make-up to represent the two communities. Use face paints to create your designs. The traditional piercings and patterns on the Yanomami faces might contrast interestingly with the piercings, make-up and tattoos on some western young people.

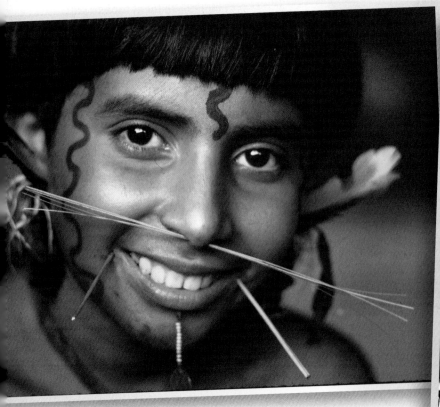

The piercings, make-up and clothing of a young Yanomami girl and a Western teenager.

Stimulus: holiday brochure

Magazines and brochures often contain advertisements that can provide stimuli for drama. Such advertisements present images of perfect people and perfect places but the reality behind some of these images can be very different. Explorative strategies can help you understand the gap between the 'ideal' and the 'real'. Look carefully at the holiday brochure image and then read some facts about the tourist industry.

Visit Paradise

Looking for peace and relaxation? This idyllic island, lined with palm beaches, is the ideal place to escape to. With sun, sea and sand, you'll find everything you need in our ideally located resorts. So don't hesitate – book online today and receive a 10% discount!

Background information

• The average British household spent nearly £2000 on holidays in 2008, 52% more than in 2001.

• Swimming pools, hotels and golf courses catering for tourists all use a lot of water. When on holiday, people use a lot more water than they do at home.

• Large cruise ships produce more than 70,000 tonnes of waste each year, which pollutes the water and kills marine life.

Try it!

This activity uses juxtaposition and explorative strategies to create meaning. The parallel scenes contrast with each other, showing different viewpoints. Think about the way in which you can use spoken language to highlight these contrasts.

	First scene	Contrasting scene
A	Create a still image representing a holiday brochure scene. Add a spoken caption.	Create a still image showing local people clearing up the rubbish left by tourists on their beach or at a special site. Add their thoughts.
B	Create a TV advert for a holiday in the destination shown above. Add a voiceover to persuade viewers of its attraction and value.	Create a TV advert for an ecotourist destination, where the culture of the people is protected and the local community has benefited from increased income from tourism.
C	Role-play a scene where a family or friends are packing for their holiday.	Role-play a scene where a group of young tourists treat a local waiter inconsiderately.
D	Create a scene where a local guide shows tourists around a sacred site.	Role-play a scene showing the tour guide remembering the site before tourism came to his village.

Reflect on the effectiveness of this drama activity:

• What did you and your class discover through this exploration work?

• Did the drama change your opinion on any of these issues?

Evaluating your work

Discuss the following questions:

- How were **voice** and **spoken language** used to convey the attitudes and viewpoint of the different cultures?
- Consider the choice of words and phrases in communicating feelings.
- How did the use of **space** and **movement** convey location?
- Were **characterisations** created through speech, gesture and movement?

Here are some notes made by a group evaluating their use of **spoken language** in the task at the bottom of page 93.

> **edexcel examiner tip**
>
> Asking questions about your work enables you and your group to understand how effective the drama has been. It can help you to see where it might be improved.

A. Caption: Is there anything more romantic than the sand beneath your feet, palm trees and unique sunsets?

> Use of rhetorical question, soft sounding words. 'Unique' implies that it is exclusive.

A. Thought: How can they treat this gift of nature, these golden sands, with so little respect?

> Again, a rhetorical question. There is a sense of disgust and of dignity.

B. Voiceover: Stroll along long stretches of idyllic beach bathed in the glorious sunshine of our exotic location.

> The language implies luxury and relaxation.

B. Travel to fragile and beautiful areas, contribute to the protection of nature's wonders and take away only memories.

> 'Fragile' is a reminder of the need to be careful. Nature and wonder are stressed to appeal to the conscience of the tourist.

C. Do you think I'll need more than two bikinis? Have we got enough sun cream – don't want to get burned!

> The usual priority of the holidaymaker is captured here.

C. Hey you! Give us another two beers…that's TWO [indicates with fingers and raucous laugh] in case you don't understand English!

> The language lacks any respect. Jokes are made at the waiter's expense. The tourist expects local people to speak his language.

D. This temple is said to be the best preserved site in our country and is dedicated to one of our gods. Magnificent carved columns hold up the roof. The walls and parts of the ceiling are decorated with gorgeous paintings .

> The importance of beliefs and the respect for the beauty of the temple are captured.

D. When I was a child this temple was a quiet place for peaceful worship. It stood majestically against the hillside and only the ox carts dragging slowly from the fields disturbed the silence.

> The implication is that tourism has created noise, traffic and building. The former peace and tranquillity are captured.

Example from a documentary response

Here is an extract from a student's documentary response to their group's practical exploration on the environment. The exploration used the stimuli of a newspaper article about a sighting of some indigenous people living in the Amazon rainforest and a variety of artefacts that contrasted the western and Yanomami way of life. The student has written an account of the exploration and sketched out a storyboard (see page 96 overleaf) to show how the group used the stimuli for dramatic exploration. As you read, think about how you can develop your own documentary response on the work you have done.

In our work on the exploitation of resources in the rainforest we focused on the newspaper article about the sighting of the Yanomami tribe and related this to the artefacts - jewellery and food. Our discussion focused on using a split-screen technique at the beginning and the end and the use of juxtaposition of images and scenes to engage the audience in the issue.

We began by showing the plane flying over the tribe: our images and dialogue showed the awe of those in the plane and the natural harmony of tribal life.

We then cross-cut from scenes of Western affluence:

- buying a burger without thought of where it has come from

- choosing cheap, tacky gold jewellery

to scenes of devastation in the rainforest:

- loggers cutting down trees

- gold miners bringing incurable diseases.

Finally we showed a symbolic image of the teenagers leaving a party, eating burgers and admiring the jewellery, which is silently watched by the tribe. Their stillness and dignified silence is a comment on Western values.

edexcel examiner comment

The written work here and the storyboard (see next page) show the use of the drama medium to realise ideas arising from the stimulus. The purpose is clear and there is justification of the decisions. There is clear evidence of understanding of certain conventions (juxtaposition, split levels) and the use of space and movement is made explicit in the storyboard. The work indicates that the candidate has engaged with the topic and is able to reflect on the meaning.

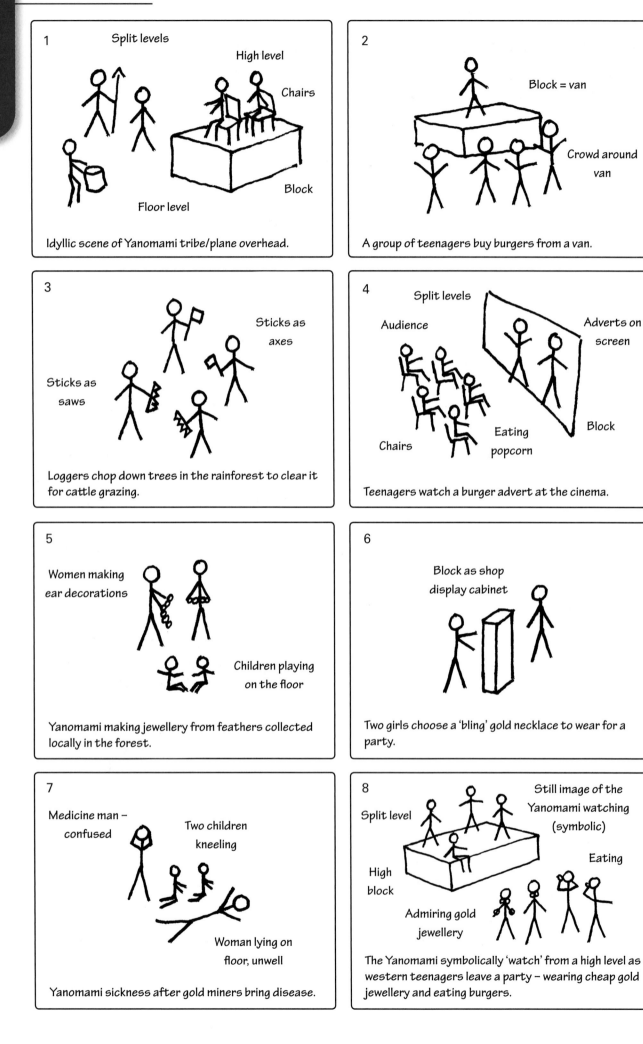

1

Split levels

High level

Chairs

Floor level

Block

Idyllic scene of Yanomami tribe/plane overhead.

2

Block = van

Crowd around van

A group of teenagers buy burgers from a van.

3

Sticks as axes

Sticks as saws

Loggers chop down trees in the rainforest to clear it for cattle grazing.

4

Split levels

Audience

Adverts on screen

Block

Chairs

Eating popcorn

Teenagers watch a burger advert at the cinema.

5

Women making ear decorations

Children playing on the floor

Yanomami making jewellery from feathers collected locally in the forest.

6

Block as shop display cabinet

Two girls choose a 'bling' gold necklace to wear for a party.

7

Medicine man – confused

Two children kneeling

Woman lying on floor, unwell

Yanomami sickness after gold miners bring disease.

8

Still image of the Yanomami watching (symbolic)

Split level

Eating

High block

Admiring gold jewellery

The Yanomami symbolically 'watch' from a high level as western teenagers leave a party – wearing cheap gold jewellery and eating burgers.

Documentary response to the practical exploration

Your documentary response is your final record of the six-hour practical exploration which you will create under controlled conditions. It can contain photographs, sketches and diagrams, but no more than 2,000 words in total.

Assessment

Your documentary response will be assessed on four main elements:

1 Your understanding of the topic

2 Your evaluation of your and others' work

3 Your use of strategies and medium

4 Your response to others and collaborative skills.

Assessment criteria	How you can demonstrate your skills
Evaluation of your understanding of the theme, topic or issue	You need to demonstrate that you understand the theme, issue or topic focused on in the practical exploration. You can do this by commenting on how your drama exploration made you think about something differently, reflecting on the issues or empathising with characters.
Evaluation of how the use of explorative strategies informed this understanding	Your work should evaluate the drama created by you as an individual, by your group and by others whose work you watched. You can do this by considering the effective use of explorative strategies and how this helped you understand the topic/theme/issue better.
Understanding of how the medium can contribute to dramatic form	You should point out your imaginative use of the drama medium and elements of drama. You can do this by indicating how you chose to interpret the stimulus and the decisions you made about form and conventions. This could be presented as an annotated diagram.
Collaborating with others and responding to their work	Your documentary response should comment on how you worked both individually and as part of the group. You should also evaluate work produced by other groups or individuals, and by the whole class. You can do this by commenting on the effectiveness of your own drama work and considering how your contribution related to other people's ideas and skills. You should also evaluate work produced by others and explain what you learned from others in your class.

Each sample exploration in this book shows different ways of exploring a topic, theme or issue using a variety of stimuli. At the end of each exploration is an example extract from a student's documentary response. These will help you see the different ways that you can present your own work.

The examiner's comments on each documentary response extract explain why the work gained a good mark.

98

Keeping a logbook

It is important to remember the detail of your six-hour practical exploration so that you can write about it in depth in your documentary response. This can be difficult, particularly if the exploration is spread over a few weeks. Keeping a logbook is a good way to record important details both during and immediately after each session.

Keep your notes short and to the point. Remember, they are just to trigger your memory when you come to writing your full documentary response. You will be able to refer to your logbook or notes when writing up your documentary response. These are the sorts of things you might want to include in your logbook:

The notes below are from a student's logbook. They were written in a 'shorthand' form very quickly during the final part of the exploration.

- Summary of initial ideas that were discussed. This could be in the form of a spider diagram (see page 73 in 'Sample Exploration 2: Tomorrow's World').

- Record how your own ideas were used and developed by the group.

- Comment on how explorative strategies were used effectively.

- Note where the drama medium and elements enhanced the work. You might want to use sketches or diagrams to show how you used the drama medium.

- Record samples of spoken language with indications of how voice was used (see page 70 in 'Sample Exploration 2: Tomorrow's World').

- Use a 'gingerbread' shape to indicate character, with notes outside showing how he/she appears to others and notes inside showing feelings and emotions (see page 88 in 'Sample Exploration 4: Stand Up for Your Rights!').

- Draw diagrams of still images and freeze frames, or take photos of them during your workshop. Add thought bubbles to note thought-tracking.

- Record briefly the evaluations made by others in your group who watched your work.

- Note your personal feelings about the meaning created in the drama.

Stimuli: Prison diary and picture of force-feeding

Strategies: Still image /thought-tracking /narration

Mediums: Sound of knocking on walls, moaning and wailing in background

– Space and levels in still image

Elements: Climax – woman is sick on doctor

– Pace and tempo – builds with each thought to climax

Narrator: Women refused to eat in prison and were force-fed because the government were afraid that one of them might die and become a martyr.

Comments on the work of others

I liked the way that the group held the still image and delivered the thought-tracking with passion. It really helped you to empathise with Mary and to feel loathing for the doctor and unsympathetic wardress. The thought-tracking of the doctor showed his antipathy to the suffragette cause and we learned how hard-hearted he was.

It was interesting that one of the wardresses, who was holding Mary down, actually had sympathy for the cause. There was a contrast with the other wardress who showed no sympathy at all. This strategy can help you to see inside the characters and reveal their feelings.

This piece helped me to realise how the suffragettes must have felt about their struggle. In the still image we saw how Mary suffered from the force-feeding. Only a very determined person would put herself through such an indignity. We take the vote for granted, a lot of women don't even bother to vote. This piece of drama made me think about how women suffered in the past so that we have the right to vote now. When I am 18 I will use it!

Writing your final documentary response under controlled conditions

- You must write your documentary response at school or college under supervision.

- The documentary response must refer to the assessed six-hour practical exploration and not to any other sessions that took place before or after this time.

- You can take your notes to the session.

- You can present your work on large pieces of paper in an imaginative way.

- There is no time limit for you to complete the documentary response. You should not take the work home or work on the final piece outside the controlled conditions.

- Your total word limit is 2,000 words. This includes continuous writing and labels for diagrams.

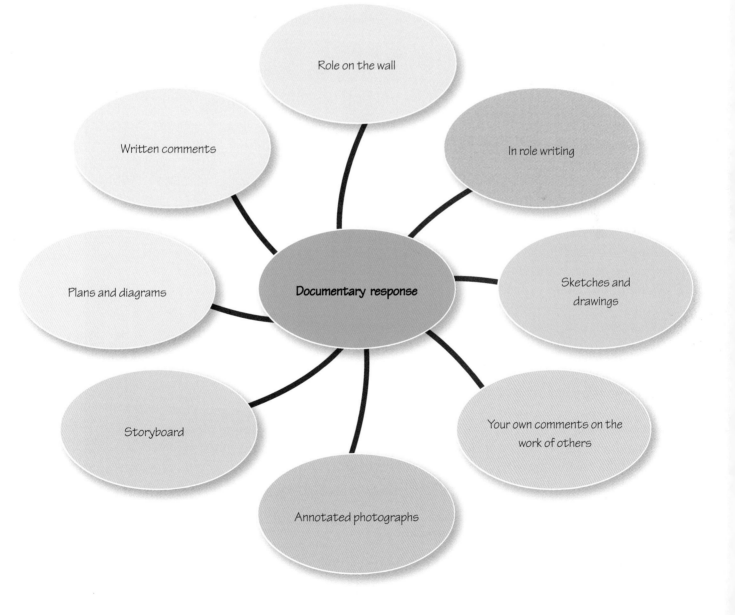

Unit 2: Exploring Play Texts

Introduction

What will you do in Unit 2?

- Explore the action, characters, ideas, themes and issues of a written play text, through a range of suggested drama activities.

- Use a range of explorative strategies, media and elements of drama to develop interpretations of the play, and gain an understanding of how it might work in performance.

- Evaluate how your exploration and use of techniques contribute to your interpretations and understanding.

- Prepare for and evaluate a live performance, drawing on the range of skills and strategies you have developed.

How are you assessed in Unit 2?

Unit 2 is worth **30%** of your total GCSE marks.

You will participate in a six-hour practical exploration of drama. This may take place on one day or be spread over a number of shorter sessions. It will take place under controlled conditions, led, supervised and assessed by your teacher. You will then write a documentary response, under controlled conditions, of up to 1000 words.

The mark your teacher gives you for this work will be based on:

- your practical work during the six-hour exploration

- your documentary response.

You will also write an evaluation of a live performance of a complete play in a maximum of 2000 words. This will be based on informal notes written after the performance. The formal evaluation will be written under controlled conditions and your mark will be based on:

- your ability to comment on a range of strategies and dramatic elements used in the performance and their effectiveness

- how well you convey and explain these ideas.

How will this book help you with Unit 2?

In this section there are five possible play texts you can explore.

They are:

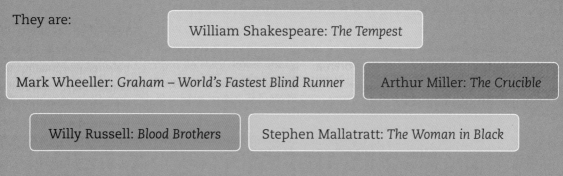

William Shakespeare: *The Tempest*

Mark Wheeller: *Graham – World's Fastest Blind Runner*

Arthur Miller: *The Crucible*

Willy Russell: *Blood Brothers*

Stephen Mallatratt: *The Woman in Black*

Each play offers exciting and interesting opportunities for you to engage with the characters, themes and storylines by developing and building on the drama skills you have. You will need to take an active and creative role, contributing ideas and analysing what you have done and learned.

Your teacher will choose the play text you will explore. If you are exploring a different play text than those covered here, you can still use the activities to develop your ability in using the Programme of Study within Unit 2. Your teacher will help you pick examples which you can adapt to suit your own work.

How do you use the Programme of Study in Unit 2?

Each play will be explored using a range of   . During these explorations you need to demonstrate your knowledge of the   and   which help to communicate the meaning of the play.

For each play there are activities (under the heading 'Try it!'), which offer different approaches to help you work on your interpretation and understanding of the play. For example, in the work on *Blood Brothers*, a   approach is suggested (see page 128) to explore alternative choices for the mother who has to make a terrible decision. By using audience intervention, you can increase your understanding of the mother's situation and how she feels at that point.

Also in this chapter there are examples of how to evaluate your use of explorative strategies. For example, you are guided on how to consider whether forum theatre gave you a better insight into parts of the play and a clearer understanding of character, in particular the mother.

In summary, the work on Unit 2 should bring together a range of approaches and elements to help you to understand the play, the playwright's intentions, and possible interpretations through performance. This will include:

- making links between the scenes you have explored and the whole play

- considering a range of different ways of viewing characters and ideas

- showing your knowledge of how playwrights, directors, designers and actors might use different approaches to present versions of the play.

What is important for success in Unit 2?

Exploring a play text successfully

During your six-hour assessment your teacher will award marks for the way you explore and respond to the chosen play. You will need to use at least four explorative strategies, at least two skill areas of the drama medium and appropriate elements of drama.

You will be assessed on:

- your understanding of the text
- your use of drama strategies, elements and medium
- how well you work with your group
- how well you communicate your understanding of plot, character, form and structure.

> **edexcel   examiner tip**
> This is not about producing a polished performance of your chosen play! It is about using the skills and strategies you have learned in the Programme of Study to explore and deepen your understanding of the play, its action, characters, themes and issues.

What is a good documentary response?

...considers how you might present your documentary response: you can produce your work in visual as well as written form.

...shows you were engaged and committed to the work on the selected play.

...evaluates the work rather than simply describing what you did during the explorations.

A good documentary response...

...uses the language of drama in your writing.

...justifies how and why you chose the explorative strategies and discusses how they deepened your understanding of meaning.

...reflects on how the drama medium, the elements of drama and the explorative strategies enabled you to understand and interpret the play.

It is important to keep detailed notes of your work on the play in a log or journal. You do not have to include all your activities in detail, but try to write notes which will prompt your memory and include specific examples of particularly effective work. You will be able to refer to these notes when you are writing your formal documentary response.

See pages 142 to 143 for more information about your documentary response.

What is a good response to a live performance?

In your response to a live performance, you will be assessed on how well you write about a performance you have seen. During the writing of this response, which will be under controlled conditions, you can refer to informal notes you made after the performance.

See pages 146 to 150 for more advice about making notes after the live performance and then writing up the formal response.

...is written in good quality English, with careful spelling, punctuation and grammar.

...comments on a range of drama elements and aspects of the drama medium, for example, how a character is portrayed on stage, what lighting is used.

A good response...

...is written in a clear, coherent style supporting points with well-chosen 'evidence' taken from the notes you made. You can be critical, provided you support what you say.

...focuses on the *effect* and *effectiveness* of these approaches and features. It is not enough simply to describe what you saw, or how you felt.

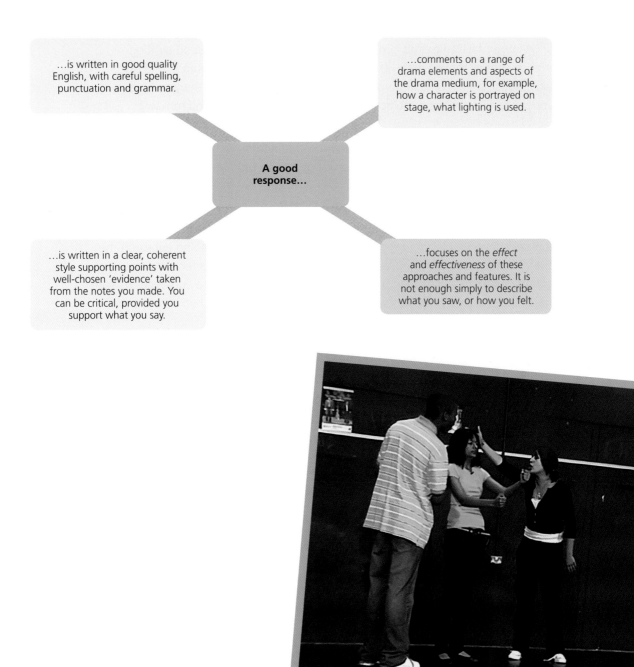

edexcel examiner tip

You will be assessed on the quality of your written work in this response, so think carefully about how clearly and fluently you express your ideas. Check your spellings, use punctuation accurately and make sure your grammar is correct.

Sample Exploration 1: The Tempest

This exploration looks at *The Tempest* by William Shakespeare.

> The play opens with a dramatic storm off the shore of a remote island. Prospero, who has magical powers, his daughter Miranda, his malformed slave Caliban and the spirit Ariel live on the island. The storm is created by Prospero, with Ariel's help, to shipwreck his enemy King Alonso and his son Ferdinand and bring them to the island.
>
> Prospero was once Duke of Milan but his brother stole his title from him, helped by King Alonso. Prospero has kept all these past events secret from his daughter Miranda and plans that she and King Alsonso's son Ferdinand will fall in love. The play explores themes of love, deception, power and forgiveness and the action of the play is both comic and romantic.

You should be familiar with the basic plot of the play and the characters involved before beginning these activities. You might want to read the text as a class, go to see the play, or watch the film.

Shipwrecked! Exploring the opening scene

The opening of a play is very important. Examining the first scene to explore ideas for staging will enable you to understand how the playwright intended to engage the audience and establish the mood and atmosphere of the production. Some plays begin quietly, introducing tensions between characters, while others draw the audience in by creating a mystery, leading the audience to listen for clues. *The Tempest* starts dramatically with a storm. Shakespeare's theatre had no electricity so technical effects were limited. He created atmosphere with words.

Try it!

- Look at the first scene and find key phrases that suggest the pandemonium and fear of the storm at sea. Each member of your group should choose a different line and think about what it means.

  Here are some examples:

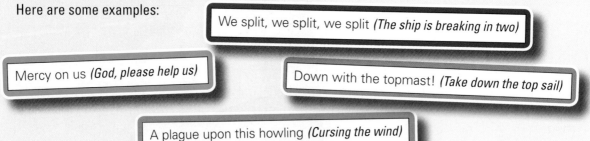

  We split, we split, we split *(The ship is breaking in two)*

  Mercy on us *(God, please help us)*

  Down with the topmast! *(Take down the top sail)*

  A plague upon this howling *(Cursing the wind)*

- Walk around the space using **vocal tone** to speak the line in different ways. Aim to create the mood of the storm as you decide how to say it.

- Agree an order in which to speak the lines: it does not need to be in the same order as they appear in the play.

- Add **movement** and the use of **levels** to show the confusion aboard the ship. How might you use your bodies to suggest elements of the ship – the masts, ropes and the movement of the ship during the storm?

- As the final line is spoken, create a still image. Use narration to create the atmosphere leading from the storm to the magical, peaceful island. Consider the drama element **contrast** when creating the difference between the frantic storm and the tranquil island.

Develop the drama using the drama medium

- Add simple staging devices, such as blocks or chairs, to create the ship.

- **Lighting** can add to the atmosphere – perhaps a blue gel to suggest darkness. If you do not have lighting in your space experiment with torches to create beams of light that move around.

- **Sound** enhances the atmosphere: experiment with vocal sound or the use of percussion. You might want to create a sound collage and record your own voices to play back later. You can also improvise with any items which are easily to hand to create appropriate sounds. Rain sticks and cymbals can be effective to create the sound of thunder. What sounds can indicate peacefulness?

Evaluation

Discuss the performances of the shipwreck scenes.

- How did you use **levels** to create the ship? Did the staging ideas add to the atmosphere? What could have been done differently to improve it?

- How did the use of **voice** suggest the fear and the chaos of the shipwreck? Think about the **tone** and **pace** of the **spoken language**.

- How did the rhythm, pace and contrasts of movement add to the scene of the storm?

- Where did the **drama medium** enhance the storm and represent the rain, thunder or darkness?

- How effectively was the **contrast** created?

Magic and monsters

In *The Tempest*, there are many magical creatures, for example Ariel who is a spirit-servant to Prospero and must do what he wants even if it involves tormenting others. Ariel doesn't want to be Prospero's servant but has a duty to him, because Prospero saved him from torment by a witch. There is also a monster, Caliban, who claims that the island is his and that Prospero has stolen it from him and made him an unwilling servant. Shakespeare, writing around 1611, was referring to how Europeans were sailing to lands that were new to them and claiming them as their own even though they were already inhabited.

Try it!

Explore the power relationship between Prospero, Ariel and Caliban. How did each character come to be on the island?

- Working in groups, create a tableau showing the characters' outer relationships, i.e. what can be seen on the surface.

- In the same group, now create a second tableau showing the characters' inner relationships, i.e. their hidden feelings about each other.

edexcel examiner tip
Do not fill the space with furniture but be selective about what is effective. Less is often more! You also need to be mindful of safety.

Playing comedy

The Tempest contains several scenes which can be explored in a comic way. The key to good comic performances is the timing of the dialogue or action: this is known as 'comic timing'. You can use the technique in the exercise below to explore a comic scene from any play.

Interpreting character

When you are working on a scripted text, you need to examine the characters that the playwright has created. Some key methods can help you to understand the roles and interpret them in your own way.

● Look at the way the character speaks. What does he or she say about other people? What are his or her opinions?

● What do other characters say about him or her? Do they all agree?

● Does the playwright indicate how the character looks and moves?

You could create a chart to record the information given by the playwright, as shown in the example below.

Character	What I say	What others say about me	How I move/look
Caliban	This island's mine … Which thou tak'st from me	Thy most lying slave … filth as thou art	hunched, crawling, sneering

Try it!

In Act 2, Scene 2, the shipwrecked Alonso and others from the ship are lost on the island. When Caliban sees Trinculo (the jester) and Stephano (the butler) he hides under his cloak. However, another storm approaches and Trinculo also gets under Caliban'ts cloak, to shelter. When Stephano arrives, he thinks he has found a four-legged monster.

The scene is very physical and depends on **action** rather than words. Read the scene in your group before trying this activity.

● Present the scene in groups of three without scripted dialogue, focusing on **movement**, **gesture** and **facial expression**.

● Now add **thought-tracking**, addressed to the audience, to add to the comedy.

Evaluation

● Why was the action amusing? What makes an audience laugh?

● How did the first activity help you to understand the humour and create comic movement?

● How did movement, gesture and facial expression add to the comic action?

● Did the thought-tracking enable you to understand how the characters were feeling?

● How did this help you find the right intonation when using the text?

● Comment on the work of another group. What was their interpretation of the scene? Do you think this is a comic scene or is it saying something else?

Using hot-seating to explore the emotions of a character

In *The Tempest*, Shakespeare reveals layers of detail about the characters. **Hot-seating** is an effective strategy to discover what a character feels. This is a very useful way for a performer to explore a distinctive approach to the role.

Try it!

- Choose two people from your group to take on the roles of Prospero and Caliban, and two people for Miranda (Prospero's daughter) and Ferdinand (King Alonso's shipwrecked son) who have fallen in love with each other.

- The remainder of the group then ask questions of the characters, who must answer in role.

- Questions in this exercise should be about feelings, not facts. For example:
  'Miranda, how did you feel when you first saw Ferdinand?'
  'Caliban, can you describe how your hatred of Prospero makes you feel inside?'

Developing role-play from a hot-seating exercise

Hot-seating enables you to think about the role. How will the discovery of emotional detail affect the presentation of the role? How can voice, movement and gesture reflect emotion? You need to apply what you have discovered to a section of the play.

Try it!

Choose a short scene which relates to some of the key questions that were asked. If the questioning of Ferdinand focused on his feelings for Miranda you might select Act 3 Scene 1, where Miranda and Ferdinand declare their love for each other.

- **Role-play** a short section – do not try to present a whole scene.

- Think about the feelings that you described in the hot-seating and explore how you can use the **drama medium**, **voice**, **movement** and **gesture** to convey these emotions in performance.

Evaluation

- How effective was the use of drama medium in conveying emotion?
- How did this strategy help you to understand the feelings of the central characters?

Exploring character relationships

The relationship between characters is a very important aspect of any play. The audience will empathise with the characters – they will take an interest in the development of romances or feel angry about a character's treatment.

Status plays a significant part in relationships. In *The Tempest* Prospero has high status because he is educated and also because he commands the island. Caliban has low status, as he is a slave. You can explore status in a play using a pack of playing cards with the 'picture' cards and Jokers removed. A 10 gives you high status whereas a 2 or 3 indicates low status (see the activity on the next page).

Try it!

Read Act 1 Scene 2, where Caliban first appears with Prospero and Miranda, from: 'Prospero: Thou poisonous slave, got by the devil himself ...' to 'Prospero: ... So, slave: Hence!'

- **Role-play** the scene with Prospero having a status of 10, Miranda a 7 and Caliban a 3.
- Think about how status affects **posture**, **movement** and **voice**.
- How can status be shown through the use of **levels** and **space**?

For example, Prospero sweeps about the space speaking in a commanding voice, whereas Caliban is hunched on a lower level and flinches in fear when Prospero comes near him. Miranda is self-assured and unsympathetic to Caliban.

Try to take different approaches when looking at text. What would happen if you tried to play this with Prospero as nervous, edgy and almost weak? What if Caliban were mocking, aggressive, unafraid?

- Explore how the scene changes when the status is different. Give Prospero a 7, Miranda a 3 and Caliban a 9.
- Play the scene again and then discuss the differences.

For example, Caliban's voice is angry and threatening and he stands up to Prospero. Miranda is afraid of Caliban and shrinks behind her father for protection. Prospero moves cautiously, showing fear that his authority is being challenged.

Evaluation

Share your work with the class and discuss the different interpretations. You might like to complete a grid like the one below.

Status: Prospero 10, Caliban 3, Miranda 7		
Use of the drama medium	**Comments and reflections**	**Sketches and diagrams**
Voice and pace/tempo	Prospero spoke in a commanding tone, speaking slowly and with emphasis on key words, e.g. 'lying slave'. His pace quickened when he ordered Caliban to fetch the fuel. Caliban's speech was slow and bitter but tinged with fear.	
Space	Miranda kept a distance from Caliban, as though he was unclean. Prospero circled Caliban in an imposing way. Caliban scurried out of the way, avoiding Prospero.	
Levels	At key moments Prospero stood very close to Caliban, looking down at him. Caliban crawled along the floor, cowering as though he expected to be struck.	
Movement and gesture	Miranda waved Caliban away with disdain when he approached her. Prospero used his magic staff grandly as he swept around the space with authority.	
Evaluation	The status helped us to play the role with conviction. When we were thinking about our status the movements, vocal tone and use of space seemed more natural.	

You can explore relationships in this way for other scenes from this play, or for any other text that you are studying. Remember that relationships depend on what the characters feel about each other and how they interact. The performance should be motivated by the character's feelings: consider the use of space and levels, the way you use your voice, movement and gesture.

Prospero (left) and Caliban in a production of The Tempest at the Almeida Theatre

Plot, action and themes

There are a number of intertwining plots in *The Tempest*:

- Prospero's capture of and revenge/forgiveness towards his enemies, including Alonso
- the conspiracy of Caliban with Trinculo and Stephano against Prospero
- the development of the love between Ferdinand (Alonso's son) and Miranda.

Each of these storylines helps to:

- establish/develop character
- move the story on (i.e. new events or information are revealed)
- create an impact on the audience (make us laugh, move us, make us feel fear, etc.).

The exercise below can help you to explore the **plot** of a play by giving each section a title and then creating an image that shows the key events.

Try it!

- Working in groups of four or five, take an act of the play.
- Discuss your act and decide on five **still images** that capture the action.
- One member of the group is the **narrator** who will tell the story of the image.
- The others play characters in the still image and speak short lines in role – they can be funny!
- Work on the transition between the still images.

Act 3

Image 1: Ferdinand carrying logs, Miranda gazing adoringly at him, Prospero secretly watching

Narrator: As Prospero's slave, Ferdinand has to carry logs.

Ferdinand: Blimey! These logs are heavy!

Narrator: Miranda is falling in love with him.

Miranda: He's really fit!

Narrator: Prospero watches secretly. He is pleased that they are falling in love.

Prospero: Excellent, they've got it bad!

- Present the acts in order and discuss how this exercise helped you to explore the **plot** and **action** of the play.

Detailed exploration: Prospero on trial

Once you understand the plot and relationships, you can consider ways of exploring the text or themes further. One way is to take the characters out of the play into a new context in order to explore the theme of justice.

The Charge

Prospero – you are charged on three counts of cruelty; first, that you kept your daughter's past hidden from her; second, that you took control of the island from its rightful owner, Caliban, and enslaved and tortured him; third, that you used a creature of the spirit world, Ariel, for your own goals and to torture others.

- In groups of five take on the roles of the following characters – Prospero, Caliban, Miranda, Ariel and Ferdinand, who will act as judge.
- Use the strategy of **hot-seating** as Prospero is cross-examined in turn by Caliban, Miranda and Ariel, and asks his own questions in return.

You will need to:

- research your role, ensuring you are clear about what happened to you
- decide on the questions you want to ask.

For example:

> **Caliban asks:** Why did you think you had the right to take my island from me?
> **Miranda asks:** What right did you have to keep me from the real world when I was growing up?
> **Ariel asks:** You promised me freedom, why did you break your promise and keep me as your servant?

Ferdinand will need to have a sense of the bigger picture – Prospero's behaviour as a whole, and also what questions to ask of the other characters. For example:

> **Ferdinand asks Ariel:** If you had not been freed by Prospero you would still be imprisoned in the tree. Don't you think that you owe him anything?

The trial can be run in your small groups, or the groups can join together with several Prosperos and other characters being questioned or cross-examined.

Developing the activity

A number of additional elements can be introduced as part of, or alongside, the trial. For example:

- Short performed sections from the play which can act as 'evidence' of how justice is a theme in the play (for example, Prospero's speech to the spell-bound Alonso and his companions in Act 5 Scene 1).

- Flashbacks/out-takes from the play such as Prospero's overthrow as Duke of Milan, or his arrival on the island and freeing of Ariel.

- Expert witnesses (from outside the play), e.g. a lawyer explaining what 'justice' means.

- Mimes which represent significant moments from the play.

Evaluation

Discuss how successful the hot-seating activity was. Think about:

- how the trial/hot-seating worked, what you said and whether you were able to remain in role

- the lines, phrases and 'evidence' you found to support your character's view of things

- how the particular approach (hot-seating) in the trial, and the activity as a whole helped you understand the action, characters and key issues or themes

- whether your view of your character (and other people's characters) changed as a result of the process.

Example from a documentary response

Here's part of a response from a student who worked on a similar task to the one described.

> Hot-seating was a real challenge but I felt it really heightened our overall understanding of the play for several reasons. First it made you think about the play itself, because your answers had to fit in to the plot and relationships. Also you had to think about motives as well as actions – for example why Prospero hadn't told Miranda about who she was earlier.
>
> Finally I felt that hot-seating really heightened our understanding of our characters and hence the text, because some of the questions asked of us were not given directly in the text – for example Prospero's relationship with his brother before he was deposed. This meant that we in the hot seat had to know our character's feelings towards the other characters and motives for certain events well enough to be able to predict what the characters would say for those particular questions. This really helped us to analyse our characters and also helped us to get inside their heads. This is why, although completely terrifying ... I feel that hot-seating was an extremely effective explorative strategy to use for this session.

edexcel examiner comment

Excellent understanding of use of strategy, and some in-depth analysis. Some reference to personal experience/evaluation could bring this up to top level.

Sample Exploration 2: Graham – World's Fastest Blind Runner

This exploration looks at the play *Graham – World's Fastest Blind Runner* by Mark Wheeller.

> The play tells the true life story of Graham Salmon MBE, who as a baby lost his sight to an incurable type of cancer but went on to become a world champion athlete. Graham was listed in the *Guinness Book of Records* as 'the world's fastest blind runner' in 1976 (100 metres in 11.4 seconds). He went on to play golf and hit a famous 'hole in one' at the British Open.

You should be familiar with the basic plot of the play and the characters involved before beginning these activities.

Exploring the plot/action of the play

The plot covers the highs and lows of Graham's life – from being rejected for countless jobs to winning a gold medal in the 400 metres at the European Championships. The play illustrates the **contrasts** in Graham's life as he strives to overcome his disability. It also raises awareness of disability, encouraging the audience to question their fixed ideas.

Try it!

In groups choose five events/moments and develop a short group presentation to convey the **contrasts**. For example, you might include the scene where Graham's parents take photographs before he has his second eye operation where his eye is removed, and Graham meeting Marie, his future wife, in his last week at secondary school.

Think about how your piece can explore the way people have pre-conceived ideas about disability.

Here are some suggestions:

- Create a series of **still images**, which show the contrasts in Graham's life.
- Add narration by selecting lines from the play, considering vocal tone to draw out your meaning
- Present the still images in order of the script
- **Cross-cutting**: develop the work by using the convention of slow-motion to show Graham winning gold, with flashbacks to less happy moments from the past.

This is an example of a student's documentary response detailing the activity above.

> We presented these key events from the play as a sort of 'conscience alley' in which Graham's parents were carrying him as a baby towards a photographer. As they did so, the other events were represented by others speaking ideas aloud, like 'cheeky bleeder – pretending to be blind!'
>
> This showed us it was a play about obstacles and challenges presented by people who didn't understand and how Graham triumphed. It made me realise that we underestimate what disabled people can achieve and often fail to look beyond the disability.

Evaluation

- How did the choices of still image and narration highlight the contrasts?
- What was effective about use of space, levels and facial expression?
- What did the activity reveal about the issues explored in the play?
- Did you feel differently about the potential for achievement of disabled people after this work?

Exploring themes and ideas

Graham had to deal with people who did not understand blindness or who took advantage of him. One way to explore these attitudes is through **thought-tracking**. This strategy can help you to understand the reasons why someone holds a certain opinion or behaves in a certain way.

Independent research

Find out about famous Paralympians, such as Tanni Grey-Thompson. What did they overcome? What were their achievements? How does this help you to understand the character of Graham, his feelings and motivations?

113

Try it!

- In groups of four, reread these two short scenes from Section 3 and Section 6 of the play:

MAUD:	I can only remember one time when a sighted kid took advantage of his blindness.
JOHN:	Oy ... come here you... feel this.
GRAHAM:	He had this piece of wood and, as I touched it; he placed his hand over mine and pressed it down onto a nail sticking up out of it.
MAUD:	The boy's mother was furious!
MARK:	It's not only children who have the propensity for cruelty... much later a man bought some second hand hi-fi equipment from Graham... real top of the range audiophile stuff. He paid in tens... but told Graham it was twenties.

MARK:	Graham had a successful career, twenty-five years of which were at the Abbey National. Most customers didn't realise he was blind... and it never caused a problem... well there was always the exception...
CLIENT:	I have a query on my income tax and I'd like some advice.
GRAHAM:	Can I look at your passbook?
CLIENT:	Of course.
GRAHAM:	I won't keep you a minute. *(He goes to exit)*
CLIENT:	Can't you read them here? Is something wrong with your eyes?
GRAHAM:	Yes... I'm blind.
CLIENT:	Then get the Manager.
GRAHAM:	He's out.
CLIENT:	I don't want you taking my books away. I'll see his deputy!
GRAHAM:	I only need them for a minute.
CLIENT:	I'm not unsympathetic; I just want to be served by someone who can see.
GRAHAM:	I wanted to tell him... it's people like him who stop people like me getting jobs... and when we get one, stop us from getting on. I wanted to have a go at him... but I came in and asked Marion, our principal clerk, to see him.
MARION:	On his way out he had the cheek to say:
CLIENT:	How generous of the company to give someone like him a job!
MARION:	We couldn't do without him!

Text reproduced by kind permission of DBDA   ISBN 978 1 902843 26 1

Try it!

The scenes on the previous page show how both children and adults were cruel, took advantage of his blindness or showed prejudice.

- Explore the scenes by improvising the events, stopping the action at important moments to **thought-track** Graham and the other character (John, the hi-fi man or the Client).

  For example:

  > Hi-fi man says:
  > OK, so here's the cash ...
  > twenty, forty, sixty ...

  > Hi-fi man is thinking:
  > Bet he didn't see this coming! Ha! Ha! I'm getting it half price from the blind geezer!

- Think about how **spoken language** and **vocal tone** can indicate attitudes and reactions.

  For example, Graham's tone might sound different in the way he speaks publicly from the 'thought-tracking' voice.

  For example, in the scene in the bank:

  > Graham says (*spoken slowly and calmly*):
  > He's out.

  > Graham is thinking (*spoken crossly showing his exasperation*):
  > How dare you speak to me as if I am simple – I can't *see* but I can do my job!

- How could you use **space**, **movement** and **facial expression** to suggest the attitudes of the characters?

Evaluation

- How did tone of voice show the feelings and attitudes of the characters?
- How did thought-tracking help the understanding of the issue of attitudes?
- Did the use of space, movement or facial expression add to the impact of the scene?
- What did this work communicate about attitudes to disability?

Exploring prejudice using rhythm, pace and tempo with space/levels

The plot shows how Graham deals with obstacles in his way: often, these are people's attitudes. The opening of Section 6 is about the attitude of potential employers to Graham and their excuses not to employ him. The playwright suggests that directors should use a stylised presentation for this scene – in other words, not lots of scenes with Personnel Officers in 'real' offices but something more lively and powerful.

Try it!

In a group:

- Read the scene together, taking on the different roles (i.e. Officer 1, 2 etc.).
- Talk about how the lines can be spoken in way that would give them impact. For example, you could you make each Officer's lines overlap so that it's like a wave of rejection, or go from speedy, bullet-like delivery to Graham's words being said slowly, quietly, sadly.
- Consider *where* the Officers would be placed and how they might move.
  For example, could they all be a higher level looking down on Graham, who is offering them a (mimed) job application form.
- You could also consider other strategies, such as **still images** or **thought-tracking**, to create powerful effects in this scene.
- Experiment with the use of space and the tempo and rhythm of the scene. What impact do you want to have on an audience? How do you want them to feel when they have watched this scene?

You could sketch out your ideas first on a large sheet of paper showing movements. You could annotate the script with your group's ideas for the pace and tempo of the lines.

OFFICER 1:   Oh... oh dear ...

Sighs slowly – but is he putting it on?

ALL OFFICERS: Oh dear!

OFFICER 1:   That could be a bit difficult.

Emphasise the word 'difficult'.

GRAHAM: Why?

Short sharp word, contrasting with the officer's words, spoken with emphasis and an angry tone.

OFFICER 2:   Erm... well... the office entrance is down a small side turning. Lorries often come and go.

Spoken slowly as if unsure what to say.

Spoken more quickly as if he has suddenly thought of an excuse not to employ Graham and wants to make it sound believable.

Evaluation

- How did the way you spoke the lines affect the meaning and impact of the scene?
- Did the decisions about space and levels add to the meaning?
- What did the exploration of this scene make you think about different attitudes to disability?
- How did you communicate Graham's determination to those watching?
- Comment on the tempo and pace. How were they used to create meaning?

Exploring characterisation

The play contains a number of important characters from Graham's life, most notably:

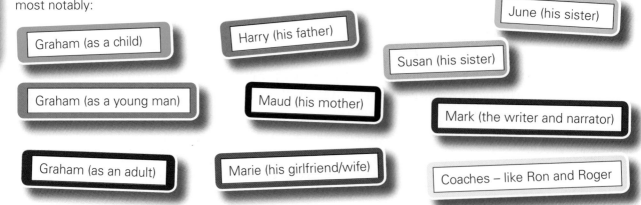

Graham (as a child)

Harry (his father)

June (his sister)

Susan (his sister)

Graham (as a young man)

Maud (his mother)

Mark (the writer and narrator)

Graham (as an adult)

Marie (his girlfriend/wife)

Coaches – like Ron and Roger

The explorative strategy of **hot-seating** helps you to find out about a character's life story, feelings and opinions.

Try it!

- Discuss the way the characters input on Graham's life (for example, the client in the bank doesn't have much affect, but Roger, the guide runner, is more significant)

- Use hot-seating to discover more detail about the characters. One way of using this strategy is to creative a TV programme showing the life of a famous person through interviews with people who know them.

- You will need a presenter (it could be one of the characters in the play or a 'neutral' presenter who is not in the play). Work on an introduction– you could do this on your own, or as a double-act with a partner. Your introduction to Graham's life should engage the audience and create interest. Consider how you might use **spoken language** and **voice** to draw in the audience. For example:

  > 'Welcome, welcome everyone to [*name of programme*] in which we present the fascinating life of a well-loved person and get comments and memories from friends and family. Tonight, we welcome a man who has...'

- Divide up the roles and research your character by completing the **role-play** card below. An example for the character of Maud, Graham's mother, is given below.

Name: Maud	Relationship to Graham: Mother
My feelings about Graham: Proud yet sorry that he never saw any of the people who loved and admired him	**One question I would like to ask Graham:** Which of your successes are you most proud of and why?
Significant moments from his life I was involved in: • The operation to remove his eye • His exclusion from school for gambling • His wedding • Getting to the final of the 400 metres. • Breaking the world record	**One question I would like to ask someone else:** I would like to ask the 'hi fi man' if he is proud of what he did?

- Run the programme scene as an improvisation, once you have developed your chosen character. You will need to make sure you have thought about how your character moves and speaks.

Here is one possible structure for your improvisation, but you can also invent your own.

1	Audience (characters) enter and take places in seats on one side, or in a circle.
2	Presenter appears in spotlight and does introduction.
3	A series of photographs (still images) highlight Graham's life (you could use the sequence from the first task of this sample exploration).
4	Graham's name is mentioned and Graham (as an adult) enters.
5	Presenter introduces each person in turn, then asks them questions to reveal their memories of Graham.
6	Graham answers – this could involve cross-cutting back to scenes from his past, like running a video film.
7	Family and friends (students in role) ask Graham their prepared questions. The presenter 'chairs' this discussion.
8	Sequence ends with Graham's 'proudest moment' – a still image or mimed sequence of him getting his MBE, or winning the 400 metres gold.

Evaluation

- How did you develop the role?
- How effective was the use of this hot-seating strategy as an exploration of Graham's life?
- What did you learn about the other characters in the play?
- How were other strategies, mediums and elements used to draw out relationships, characters and key issues in this activity?

The race! Exploring strategies for staging

The race at the end of *Graham,* where he won a gold medal in the European Championships, presents an exciting challenge. Presenting large-scale events on stage requires inventive use of drama forms. In a play by David Hare, *The Permanent Way,* a dramatic train crash was represented using sound and a back projection of the approaching train.

The race as staged by a youth group for the creation of a DVD of the play

Try it!

- Discuss in a group how you could present the race.
- Consider the **strategies**, aspects of the **drama medium** and **elements of drama** that you could employ in exploring this scene. For example, **cross-cutting**, **still images**, **narration** (strategies), **lighting**, **music**, **sound** (mediums), and slow motion (element).
- Think about the intended impact of the scene. How can you build tension and create the atmosphere of the race?
- Present the work.

Evaluation

- How effective were the choices of strategies, medium and elements in solving the staging challenges?
- What impact did the realisation have on those watching?
- What suggestions would you make for improvement? Would you stage it differently if you had more professional technical equipment?

Examples from documentary responses

Below are three extracts from work on the final race sequence of *Graham* by different students.

● Identify the drama strategies employed by the students.

● Consider how well the students refer to the language of drama.

● Identify how well they comment on the effect of the choices they made.

Then, match the extracts to the examiner's comments that follow – which is which?

Student A

> We did a thought tunnel of Graham. This was to show what his character was like and what people thought of him. Andy represented Graham and ran in slow motion down the lines of the class. The first time we said things that we thought would go on in his head. This was like 'I'm going to win', 'I can do anything I put my mind to' but the second time we were saying things that other people had said and lots of them were nasty, 'You can't see what you're doing.' It made me feel that Graham must have been really special to overcome all that nastiness. He was a real winner.

Student B

> For staging the final race the most important thing was to put across the energy and the achievement but to have everyone running around the stage would have been too chaotic and messy and the proxemics would have been a nightmare. We liked the idea of the runners in slow motion because you can show effort like in slow mo re-runs of races when the runner's face is distorted with puffed out cheeks and agonised expressions. This worked very well because you could really see the effort and progress of the race, but it didn't really show energy or the excitement. So we decided to contrast the slow movement with a very fast commentary from two members of the crowd. This also linked in with the narrative technique of the play.

Student C

> We staged the race in slow motion. This was so that the audience could keep track of where Graham was. He started a bit at the back but slowly came to the front. This was to build tension so that the audience would not know at first if he won or not. His facial expression looked like it was a great effort until the end. He pumped his arms slowly up and down to look like he was running, and at the end he raised them in victory as he crossed the line. This was to show the audience he had won. Two narrators narrated the race at the same time saying things like 'he's at the first bend, he's overtaking'. Getting faster and more excited as it got to the end. This was to show the speed of the race because the movement was in slow motion. This worked well because it was a contrast to the running and the crowds do get that excited at a race.

edexcel ⠿ examiner comment

High-level analysis

Creative ideas linked to the drama medium and elements and interpretation of text with considerable understanding. Fluent use of language of drama.

edexcel ⠿ examiner comment

Mid-level analysis

Ideas are apparent in the description but analysis and evaluation are limited and need to go further, explaining reasons for choices and effect of these.

edexcel ⠿ examiner comment

Low- to mid-level analysis

Largely descriptive but with some limited justification of drama strategies used. Needs more depth of analysis such as an evaluation of outcome and relationship to text.

Sample Exploration 3: The Woman in Black

This exploration looks at the play *The Woman in Black* by Stephen Mallatratt, a chilling thriller for two actors, based on a novel by Susan Hill.

The play tells the story of Eel Marsh House, where the young solicitor Kipps is sent to deal with the house of an elderly widow, Alice, who has just died. Once there, he encounters the ghost of 'the woman in black'. When the woman in black – Jennet – was alive, she was pressured to give up her son Nathaniel for adoption because she wasn't married. Her married sister, Alice, adopted him. Jennet planned to take him away with her but when the day came, the boy was out in a pony and trap and was involved in an accident where he and the driver drowned in the marshes. Her spirit has been seeking revenge ever since. Whenever the Woman in Black appears, a child has died somewhere.

You should be familiar with the basic plot of the play and the characters involved before beginning these activities.

Exploring the conventions of a thriller

Plays can be categorised into **genres** which tell us something about content and style. For example, the genre of tragedy will often be dark and contain elements which convey strong emotion. The documentary genre will be formal and factual and the genre of comedy amusing. When you think about the genre of a play, you need to consider the conventions that you would expect to find.

Key term
• **genre**

Try it!

The Woman in Black is described as a thriller or ghost story. The central character describes the story as being about 'haunting and evil, fear and confusion, horror and tragedy' (Kipps).

In groups, create a spider diagram or mind map describing what you might expect from this type of play. Think about the drama medium – e.g. set, lighting, sound, costume, voice and language. The diagram below has been started for you.

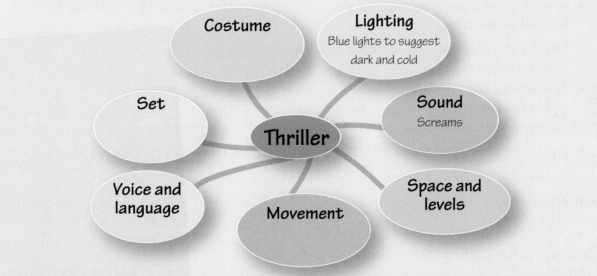

This activity can be used for any text that you are studying. It helps you to explore your first reactions to the genre. You can revisit the diagram throughout your exploration to check whether these initial ideas are helpful in your understanding of the text.

Independent research

In *The Woman in Black*, an ageing solicitor, Kipps, tells his story to an actor as a desperate attempt to exorcise the ghosts of the past. Kipps and the actor act out the story in an old Victorian theatre.

- What would a Victorian theatre look like? The playwright gives some indication when he describes gilding and cherubs. Find out about other features of this style of theatre. How does this setting contribute to the atmosphere of the play?

- Notice how the Actor refers to the theatre's sound system on page 8: this reminds the audience that they are watching a play about a play. This idea of a 'play within a play' is known as **meta-theatre**. Another example of this is in Shakespeare's *A Midsummer Night's Dream* when the mechanicals perform their play. Do you know of any other examples?

Examining the plot using still image and sound

Selecting the key moments from a play text can help you to consolidate your understanding of the plot.

Key terms
- **soundscape**
- **meta-theatre**

Try it!

You can do this exercise at the start of your exploration if you have read the whole play, or leave it until the end if you are exploring the text in sections.

- In groups of five or six, decide on five dramatic moments from the play – for example, when Kipps saves the dog, Spider, from sinking in the mud.

- Create a **still image** for each moment. Consider:
  — use of space and levels
  — facial expression
  — eye contact
  — gesture.

- Give each still image a title. One person speaks this with appropriate vocal tone.

- Now add **vocal sound** to establish the atmosphere, e.g. hissing to create the sound of the eerie marshes (**soundscape**).

- Each member of the group should make a different sound but not necessarily continuously.

- Bring the image to life, like a silent movie, exaggerating the movements and gestures, playing against the background of the soundscape.

- Present the still images and consider the transition between them.

Evaluation

- How effective was this exercise in presenting the story clearly?

- Comment on the quality of the still images.

- What did the soundscape add to the atmosphere?

Kipps visits Eel Marsh House

Exploring the fear in the village of Crythin Gifford

The play tells the story of events in this village where residents were terrified by the Woman in Black. In this exercise, you will explore the fear and suspicion of the villagers. **Narration** is an important aspect of the play, with Kipps telling the story to both the Actor and the audience.

- Working as a whole group discuss how the villagers felt about the events of Eel Marsh House. Each person takes on the role of a villager. Make sure that you do not all become similar characters by announcing who you are before you begin.

- Move around the space individually or in pairs (for example, if you are mother and child), showing your anxiety through physicality, facial expression and dialogue.

- Now create a 'walk-in' **still image**. Move into the space one at a time, gradually building up a picture of the village in fear.

- Develop the activity by adding narrative. Discuss ideas in the group. One of you now becomes the **narrator** who describes the scene, comments on individuals and creates the atmosphere of dread through **spoken language** and **vocal tone**.

- You can add to the mood of this piece through **lighting**.

Evaluation

- How did your facial expression and posture suggest how you were feeling?

- Comment on how the narrator's voice and spoken language suggested fear.

- What was effective about the creation of the village by the whole class?

Exploring the convention of multiple role-play through the use of the drama medium

You are probably familiar with one performer playing a number of different characters in a piece of drama. Actors use various techniques to convey different roles effectively, including voice, movement, costume and props. In *The Woman in Black*, two people portray numerous characters without ever leaving the stage to change costume or apply make-up.

Try it!

- In the centre of the space place a large box or basket containing a variety of hats, scarves, pieces of material and small props.

- In turn, go to the box and take out one item. Using this item **role-play** one of the characters from the play. Think about how you speak and move as this character and how you will use the prop. The remainder of the class must comment on how well the character was presented.

- In pairs, select one of the stories from the play. One person plays Kipps and the other the Actor. Use items from the box and rehearse the scene using the play text. Focus on **voice**, **movement** and **characterisation**. Your task is to make the roles totally convincing though use of the props you have available.

Evaluation

- Note one or two features of the roles you played

- How did you use voice and movement to establish character?

Using hot-seating to explore minor roles and silent characters

All the characters in a play have an important function. The smaller roles have less dialogue but provide important insights into the plot and the central characters. You can explore these roles by **hot-seating** them. Asking well-chosen questions that encourage imaginative responses can provide the 'backstory'.

Try it!

1. Keckwick takes Kipps to Eel Marsh House in his pony and trap. Towards the end of the play, we discover that he is the son of the trap driver on the day of Jennet's son Nathaniel's death.

   - Choose someone to become Keckwick, who answers in role.
   - The rest of the group ask questions which reveal information about Alice (Jennet's sister) and the pony and trap accident where Keckwick's father died.
   - Discuss as a group what you have created this exercise.
   - How might this help you to understand Keckwick's actions in the play?

2. The Woman in Black does not speak and she is not listed as a character. Perhaps the playwright wants the audience to wonder whether they too have seen a ghost in the theatre.
   This exercise uses **hot-seating** and the drama medium of **lighting** to establish the atmosphere while exploring the woman's motivation and emotion.

   - Look at the play and re-read the moments when the woman appears. What is the dramatic effect of her appearance at these key moments?
   - One person becomes Jennet (the Woman). If possible, he or she should wear a black cloak or other suitable clothing.
   - You need a torch and blackout facilities. Sit in a circle and leave an empty chair. Turn off the lights.
   - The Woman in Black enters with the torch held under her chin: this gives a sinister impression. She sits silently on the chair ready to answer questions.
   - Hot-seat the Woman in Black to explore her grief and desire for revenge.

Evaluation

- What did you learn about the characters from the hot-seating exercises?
- How might this information help you to present these characters?

Harnessing the imagination

The play depends on the audience being able to picture the various locations. A wicker trunk and a few chairs suggest a desk, a pony and trap and a train carriage.

In the play, Kipps speaks to the audience:

> **Kipps** *(as Keckwick)*: And so, imagine if you would, this stage an island, this aisle a causeway running like a ribbon between the gaunt grey house and the land.

This **convention** requires the audience to 'suspend their disbelief'. This means that the playwright is asking the audience to forget that they are in a theatre and that they are watching two actors pretending that a wicker trunk is a train carriage. Instead, the audience is encouraged to use their imagination along with the actors.

Try it!

- Working in groups of four use a stage block or a chair in as many different ways as you can to suggest locations. Include spoken language and mime to create meaning.
- Share some of these and discuss why they were effective.

A wicker basket becomes a train carriage in a London production of the play

Creating tension and dramatic impact

The important feature of *The Woman in Black* is that the audience must believe completely in what they are seeing, otherwise it will not be effective as a thriller.

Try it!

- In groups of five read on page 48 from 'in the sequence snatches of dialogue return' to 'Then she is gone' on page 50, about Kipps and the horror of the Woman in Black.
- Look carefully at how the **language** of the stage directions creates the mood and atmosphere.
- Create Kipps' nightmare using sound and voices. You can add lighting to add to the atmosphere.
- In your group one person becomes the Actor, who narrates the story from 'There is only one last thing left to tell', and one person becomes the Woman in Black. The rest of the group add sounds to create the atmosphere and **climax**. These sounds might be vocal (controlled eerie screams, hissing or percussion – drum, rain stick, triangle). Consider how you can create the sound of the pony's hooves.
- Work on this scene, experimenting with the strategies and drama mediums to create the mood of terror using voice (Actor), movement (Woman) and sound (group).
- **Mark the moment** when the Woman in Black appears. Think about the most effective way to communicate this important event to an audience.

Evaluation

- How did the use of the drama medium suggest the horror of the event?
- How did you use the drama medium to mark the moment when the Woman in Black appeared?
- Give two examples of the effective use of sound and movement in building tension.
- What did you learn about the creation of theatrical tension through this work?

Creating a design for *The Woman in Black*

The challenge for a designer is to provide a set that can be used for many different purposes. The designer of the London production, Michael Holt, captured the eeriness of Eel Marsh House as well as enabling the actors to be inventive with the few items of furniture. One of the most impressive features of Holt's design is the nursery that exists behind the gauze at the back of the stage: when covered in white sheets it is believably a graveyard full of headstones.

Try it!

- In your drama space, experiment with the creation of the graveyard in the scene on pages 26–27. Lower the lights and, if possible, add some stage lighting with blue gels. Torches can be very effective if you do not have access to lighting.
- Position blocks, tables and chairs in the space and cover them with white sheeting. Notice how the colour changes in different lights.
- Work on presenting this scene, where Kipps sees the woman in the graveyard, experimenting with the lighting and use of space. You might also want to use back projection.
- Note how the medium of sound adds to the atmosphere.

Evaluation

- Discuss the theatrical effect of these simple devices.
- What was the most spine-chilling moment in this scene? Why?
- How effective was the drama medium in creating mood and atmosphere? Share your designs with the group and discuss this. What effect did the combination of performance and set have on those watching?

'Then I looked up ahead and saw as if rising out of the water itself, a tall, gaunt house of grey stone with a slate roof.'

Examples from documentary responses

In our group we devised a series of still images to tell the story of *The Woman in Black*. We then brought these images to life, adding a soundscape. The first image showed Mr Kipps at the Inn on his journey to Eel Marsh House. The student who played Mr Kipps stood some distance from the group of other actors who played the customers at the Inn showing that he was an unwelcome stranger. At the moment when we chose to stage the freeze, the actor used an expression of surprise on her face, a questioning expression towards the student playing the innkeeper, with her hands slightly open and her brow creased. This showed Mr Kipps' confusion at the reaction to "Eel Marsh House". When we brought this image to life and added the soundscape of the customers chattering which suddenly stopped after Mr Kipps had spoken, an atmosphere of tension and suspense was created. We decided to use a tick-tock sound created by the whole group as we re-positioned ourselves, in order to make the transition to the next still image smoother. It also created a feeling of time running out for Mr Kipps and each time we created the tick-tock sound, we made the pace of this a little faster to add to this tension.

edexcel examiner comment

There is a clear description of the practical activity and of how the students developed this.

The student analyses the effects created, explaining how drama mediums of use of space, facial expression and pace, were used.

One way that we explored the character of the Woman in Black was through hot-seating so that we could discover more about her 'back-story'. We used a torch to light the face of the actor playing Jennet and a black cloak to cover her clothing – these added a sense of reality and mystery to the character to begin with. Some of the questions that we asked included quite dramatic, emotional questions such as, "You obviously loved your son very much? Why did you agree to give him up?" The actor playing Jennet reacted very emotionally to this, screaming and almost crying as she said "I never agreed to give him up, never! They made me, they MADE me – don't you understand? THEY MADE ME!" As she said "they made me" over and over again, her voice got higher and the volume also became louder and louder which suggested her emotions were running very high. She moved off the chair, and keeping the torch focussed on her face, she got closer to the students questioning her, almost as though she was threatening each of them. She then sank back on the chair and hid her face in her hands as though she was too upset to speak. This made the hot-seating a much more realistic experience as we all connected with Jennet's anger and grief, as well as seeing her as quite an intimidating character.

edexcel examiner comment

Again, a very clear description of the hot seating strategy and how it was used here.

The student analyses the effects created by the use of lighting and costume and the student's ability to stay in role. There is very clear analysis of use of voice and the effect this created as well as understanding of character.

Sample Exploration 4: Blood Brothers

This exploration focuses on *Blood Brothers*, a play/musical written by Willy Russell in the mid-1980s.

> The play tells the story of twins who are separated soon after birth and brought up in very different families. Mickey is kept by his mother Mrs Johnstone, but the woman she cleans for, Mrs Lyons who is childless, brings up Eddie. As they grow up, it happens that they become friends without knowing they are twins. At times the play is very funny but there is also tragedy as their relationship involves twists and turns, ending with their tragic death.

You should be familiar with the basic plot of the play and the characters involved before beginning these activities.

Using still imaging and narration to explore plot and themes

One way of exploring the plot of a play is to use **narration** to present your own retelling of the story. A key character in *Blood Brothers* is the Narrator, who tells the story and interacts with the other characters.

Try it!

- In groups of five or six select a section of the play. Make sure that the whole play is covered by the different groups in your class.
- Reread your section and pick out what you think are the significant moments or events. Give each moment a title that summarises the action. Create a series of **still images** for these moments linked by the **narrator**.
- Work with your group to put your still images and narrations together, so that you retell the story of the play in a seamless manner. For example:

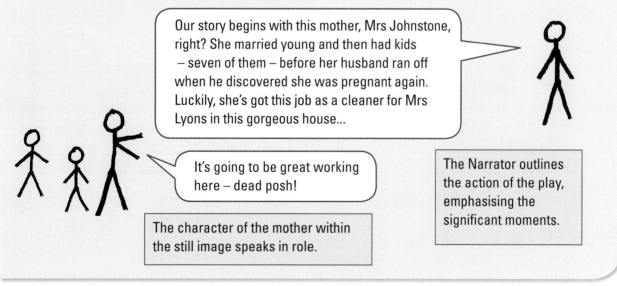

Our story begins with this mother, Mrs Johnstone, right? She married young and then had kids – seven of them – before her husband ran off when he discovered she was pregnant again. Luckily, she's got this job as a cleaner for Mrs Lyons in this gorgeous house...

It's going to be great working here – dead posh!

The Narrator outlines the action of the play, emphasising the significant moments.

The character of the mother within the still image speaks in role.

Evaluation

- How did the use of the strategies still image and narration help you see how your section fitted into the overall plot?
- Which significant moments did you choose, and why did you think they were important?

Exploring characters' motivations: forum theatre

Key term
• dramatic irony

Powerful dramas such as *Blood Brothers* always involve choices – people making decisions for good or for bad. Sometimes the audience knows what the result of those choices will be because they have better information than the characters: this is known as **dramatic irony**. On other occasions, the audience doesn't know how things will turn out. **Forum theatre** is a useful way of exploring choices that characters make in a play.

edexcel ▦ examiner tip

Dramatic irony is very significant in *Blood Brothers*. For example, every time that Mickey and Eddie meet, the audience knows they are real brothers, but they don't. This creates tension and you'll have to work out how to deal with this. Is the effect of the tension humorous, or perhaps sad? How will you communicate this to people watching?

Try it!

The Mother's decision to give up one of her twins is a key moment in the play. Explore her motivations and her relationships with other characters using **forum theatre**.

- Two people begin by acting out Act 1 Scene 5 (Mrs Lyons and Mrs Johnstone).

- The student playing the Mother can stop when she feels she doesn't really have an answer to Mrs Lyons' arguments.

- At this point, one of the observers suggests an answer or statement she could make to counter Mrs Lyons. For example:

> **Mrs Lyons:** ... if he's with me, you'll still be able to see him each day as you come to work.
>
> **Suggestion:** Tell her that will be more difficult – it will just make it harder ...
>
> **Mother:** That will be more difficult, Mrs Lyons – it will just make it harder ...

- The improvisation then continues and the observers can stop the action to make suggestions at any time.

Evaluation

- Discuss the interventions. What was suggested? How did this change the course of the scene?

- How did this exploration help you gain an understanding of Mrs Lyons' motives and emotions?

- Did this exploration change your view of these characters?

Understanding themes, character and spoken language through cross-cutting

Class, social background and power are three of the main themes of *Blood Brothers* and are reflected in the way the characters speak. Read the lines from the play given below and compare the language in the boxes on the left with those on the right. What does the language reveal about the characters?

I was dead worried about having another mouth to feed.

Your work has deteriorated. We're just not happy with it.

Mam our Sammy's robbed me other gun and that was me best one!

Shall I tell Daddy to telephone for the doctor?

Cross-cutting between two scenes in a play can help you explore relationships between characters and how these develop during the course of the play. In *Blood Brothers*, the playwright uses this technique to highlight the differences in social class at key moments in the play:

● the Policeman's visit to the families following the window-breaking

● the contrast between the public school that Eddie attends and Mickey's comprehensive.

Try it!

Use **cross-cutting** to play the following two scenes together: Act 2 Scene 2 (from '**Mickey**: Gis a sweet' to '**Mickey**: I don't know. It sounds good though, doesn't it?') and Act 5 Scene 1 (from 'Eddie, now a bright young executive' to the end of the scene). These scenes emphasise the breakdown in relationship between Eddie and Mickey.

● Begin with some lines from the Act 2 Scene 2 extract, freeze the action, and then include some dialogue from the Act 5 Scene 1 extract.

● **Cross-cut** to the early scene and end with a significant moment from the final scene.

● Consider how you can create a **climax** or **anti-climax**.

● Think about the role **spoken language** plays (in particular the **choice of words** the writer uses), not just to convey character, but also to convey humour and dramatic irony.

Evaluation

● How did cross-cutting emphasise the theme or meaning and help you understand the changing relationship between Eddie and Mickey?

● How did the group create climax or anti-climax?

● What was the effect on those watching the scene?

Developing characterisation using hot-seating and narration

In many ways, we could describe *Blood Brothers* as a modern tragedy. In *Blood Brothers* we could say that everyone suffers. But who, if anyone, is to blame for what happens? The task below uses a variation on **hot-seating** to explore the part different characters play in contributing to the events that take place.

Task: CSI Liverpool

Work in a group to develop a prepared improvisation. You will need to have the following roles in your group:

- Detective Chief Inspector (DCI; also a narrator for these purposes)
- Crime Scene Investigator (CSI)
- Mother, Mrs Johnstone
- Mr Lyons
- Mrs Lyons
- Linda, Mickey's wife (Eddie and Linda also have a relationship)
- Two 'bodies' (Mickey and Eddie – to be removed shortly after the scene begins)

Stage 1: Set up a **still image** of the moment minutes after Mickey and Eddie are killed in the climax to the play and have fallen to the ground – the scene the DCI and CSI might come across when they arrive. Remember to use space and levels effectively.

Stage 2: The DCI as **narrator** moves around the still image, describing who each person is and making observations about the scene (as if in a photo for an inquest). The CSI will also be present and could be taking photos. As the DCI moves around, he or she should ask for the camera to focus on each person – their face, body, etc. – in turn.

Stage 3: Interrogation rooms. Now set up a series of interrogations – this will involve using **hot-seating** to question each character. You may decide to have each character interrogated individually or to combine some of the interviews. The purpose of the interviews is to investigate who is to blame for the deaths.

Stage 4: Confession. The improvisation will end with each character (Mother, Mr Lyons, Mrs Lyons, Linda) performing a short monologue of their own devising direct to the audience. This can be prepared in advance – or can be spontaneous. Mickey and Eddie could speak as ghosts from beyond the grave, revealing their true feelings about what has happened and who they blame.

In groups, re-enact the final scene, drawing on your still image, narration, hot-seating and monologue work to inform this.

Evaluation

- How effectively did the group use space and levels?
- Comment on the facial expression and reaction of the silent characters.
- What did the DCI and CSI find out in their interrogations? Discuss how effectively spoken language was used to describe the scene.
- How did hot-seating and monologue help you to explore the characters in more depth?
- Did your views about any of the characters or the events of the play change as a result of this exercise?

Exploring a scene in detail using mime, movement, marking the moment and the drama medium

There are two characters who lose their sanity in this play: Mrs Lyons and Mickey. Mrs Lyons is unbalanced by her fear that Eddie will discover the truth that Mickey is his twin, whereas Mickey suffers from depression when he is in prison as a result of a burglary and struggles to recover after his release.

edexcel examiner tip

Playing madness on stage is very challenging: it is important to maintain the truth of the character and not to exaggerate to the point where the performance becomes comic.

Try it!

Read the following two scenes again:

'High on the hill the mad woman lives' (about Mrs Lyons, page 60)

'His mind's gone dancing' (about Mickey, page 74)

- How does the playwright suggest insanity?
- Why are the characters losing touch with reality?

There are similarities in the use of form in these scenes. The story is told through song or rhyme with the action mimed.

The key difference is that in Mickey's story the pace and tempo are slow, mirroring his listlessness, whereas Mrs Lyons' scene is frenzied, reflecting her hysteria. You should consider this distinction when playing the scenes.

The playwright, Willy Russell, uses Marilyn Monroe as a symbol throughout the play. She represents the decline of Mrs Johnstone and the theme of madness.

- Work in groups of five or six and choose one of the scenes.
- One member of the group could become a narrator, speaking the words of the song/rhyme, or you could play the CD of the production. The children's rhyme in Mrs Lyons' scene could be delivered as a children's chant using the whole group. Experiment with ideas before making a decision.
- Consider how to stage the scene using space and levels, mime and movement.
- Decide on one very significant moment in the scene that you want those watching to notice. Use any technique to mark the moment.

Evaluation

- What was the difference in pace and tempo between the scenes?
- How did you draw out the symbolic significance of Marilyn Monroe?
- How did you use mime and voice to create meaning?
- Comment on your use of space and levels.
- Discuss how vocal tone and choral speaking create mood.
- How effective was the strategy of marking the moment?

Developing the scene using the drama medium

Discuss how you can include the medium of drama to enhance your work. Your choice will be determined by the facilities available in your school.

You may decide that you want to use the **drama medium** to **mark the moment**, for example, with a sound or lighting effect.

- **Lighting:** The mood of the prison and Mickey's depression could be **symbolised** with blue lighting as it creates a cold and sombre mood. Take care not to light the whole space in a strong colour – try to suggest the mood subtly. Mrs Lyons' frantic movement might be punctuated with flashing lights or slowly increasing red. If you do not have stage lighting you can create the mood using torch beams or by switching off some of the overhead lights in your space.

- **Costume:** Think about how costume can reflect mood and character. Mrs Lyons' usually immaculate clothes might be slightly dishevelled. Mickey could begin the scene in prison overalls but remove them symbolically as he is released. How can costume be used to suggest the other characters?

- **Sound:** If you are speaking the song/rhyme lines, rather than playing the CD, you can add sound to highlight key moments and to create mood. A clash of a cymbal, for example, could echo Mrs Lyons' disturbed mind, or humming could accompany the monotony of Mickey's prison cell.

> **edexcel :::: examiner tip**
> It is not always necessary to have technical equipment; you can include the drama medium by being imaginative with simple effects.

Try it!

- Now choose a scene or section of the play to develop.
- Focus on the selective use of the drama medium to enhance the work by creating meaning, by drawing attention to key moments or as a symbol.
- Present the work.

Evaluation

- Comment on the use of the drama medium. How did your choices add to the meaning of the scene?
- Did this exploration change your view of the characters?

Mickey and Eddie

Examples from documentary responses

Below are two student responses to some similar work done on *Blood Brothers*. Read them and identify:

- what element or elements of drama within the play were being explored (i.e. **action/plot**, **characterisation**)
- which exploratory strategies were used (e.g. **still image**?)
- if there were any references to the drama medium (i.e. **use of set/props**, **spoken language**, etc.)

Then, in a group, discuss how effectively you think each extract explains these points.

We then went on to explore Mrs Johnstone's progression throughout the play. We explored the lyrics of the song, 'Marilyn Monroe', and we began to analyse the story they told. My group and I decided that the moment of highest tension in Mrs Johnstone's song was when her husband walked out on her: 'Me husband, he walked out on me, a month or two ago'. To portray this as the important moment in the song, we chose to freeze and stopped singing and created a still image showing the conflict within the family. We decided that the whole group would try to pull the husband back when he went towards the 'other woman', representing Mrs Johnstone's inner feelings. Then, after 5 seconds or so, the song would continue, and so would the fast pace. We opted to convey the moment in this way because we thought that pulling her husband back towards herself and the family is what Mrs Johnstone would want to do and what she wishes would happen. This created a moment of stillness and sadness within the fast pace of the song which was dramatically effective and explored the grief hidden by her busy life.

> **edexcel examiner comment**
> There is a clear description of the practical activity.

> **edexcel examiner comment**
> The student explains why this practical activity was appropriate, what effect it aimed to create and how the drama medium of pace was used.

There were a few groups which performed brilliant pieces, but one of the groups in particular stood out from the rest, which was a group that decided to show the differences between the two families, using cross cutting they showed the two mothers on a split stage and their houses one side of the stage was dirty and the other immaculate, then showed the twins one tatty, the other clean and dressed smartly which showed a good contrast between the two homes. Then they cross cut, to when they first met which showed how alike they really were which was really effective in linking the two boys.

> **edexcel examiner comment**
> The student notes that there was contrast here but could have included further detail on how this was conveyed by the actors themselves in dramatic terms.

Sample Exploration 5: The Crucible

This exploration looks at *The Crucible*, a play by Arthur Miller.

This is a play written in the 1950s about the witch trials in Salem, Massachusetts, on the east coast of America in the 17th century. Set in an authoritarian Puritan (strict Christian) society, a group of girls caught dancing and meddling with spells in the woods are accused of witchcraft. This leads to hysteria in the community. Innocent villagers are tried and hanged. The moral dilemma of John Proctor is at the heart of this dramatic play.

You should be familiar with the basic plot of the play and the characters involved before beginning these activities.

Often the title of a play can give you useful information about its themes and plot. *The Crucible* suggests chemistry: a crucible is a melting pot in which metals are heated and changed. In the play the residents of Salem undergo a change. Another meaning of 'crucible' is a severe test or trial: this suggests both the witch trials and Proctor's test of faith. The 'crucible' is broadly representative of many of the play's key elements: it is a **symbol** of what takes place.

Exploring the background to the play

The play opens with the apparent illness of Betty Parris following the incident of dancing in the woods. Outside the house, the townspeople have gathered and rumours of witchcraft are spreading. Act 1 deals with the immediate aftermath of the girls' actions. Exploring the events that provide the focus of the play's debate can help you to understand the characters' emotions and motivation.

Try it!

- Work in groups of seven, taking on the roles of the girls who experiment with witchcraft in the woods.
  — Abigail is the ringleader
  — Betty is the youngest
  — Mary Warren is the most nervous
  — Mercy Lewis is strong minded
  — Susanna Walcott
  — Ruth Putnam
  — Tituba, the black servant, who is persuaded to make spells and contact spirits.
- Use **lighting** or **sound effects** to create the mood in your drama space.
- **Role-play** the scene, considering how **spoken language** can demonstrate a character's feelings.

Here is a short extract from one group's work which they recorded:

Abigail: You're a coward Mary, come closer and stop looking so terrified.

Mary: Abby, this is wrong we'll be punished if we are caught.

Mercy: Can Tituba really call up the spirits of the dead?

Tituba: Don't make me do it, Abby, if they catch us I'll be whipped.

Abigail: Come here all of you! Look into the cauldron – concentrate – what can you see?

(The girls hold hands and hum in a low tone. The humming grows louder and more frantic. Tituba begins to sway, making sweeping movements over the cauldron with her arms.)

Note: The cauldron is called a 'kettle' in the text.

Evaluation

● How did you use the *drama medium* (particularly **sound**, **spoken language** and **movement**) to create the mood and signify emotion?

● How did this activity help you to understand the feelings of the characters at the start of the play?

● Why do you think the playwright Arthur Miller chose to begin the play at this point, after something dramatic had already taken place?

Using narration and role-play to develop understanding of plot

One way of familiarising yourself with the plot of a play is to use **narration** and **role-play**.

Try it!

- Work in groups of three as Abigail, Mary Warren and a narrator.

- **Role-play** a scene where Abigail confronts Mary Warren after they have run away from the woods. Abigail threatens Mary because she thinks that Mary will tell the truth about what happened. Abigail intends to invent a lie.

- The narrator comments on the action, rather than simply telling the story.

- To begin to empathise with the characters and the environment of the play you could try to imitate the language and style of Miller's characters.

Here is an example:

> ABIGAIL: *(grabbing Mary's cloak as she flees from the woods)* You speak of this in the Proctor house and you will feel the weight of my wrath on your head, Mary Warren. You be a terrible coward.
>
> MARY: *(shaking off Abigail's grasp)* Leave me alone, Abby! I did nothing. Why should I be blamed? You made us do it Abby!
>
> NARRATOR: Mary Warren wants to escape punishment but will her fear of Abigail be too great? Abigail is a strong character – all the girls fear her.

You could use this exercise with other characters. For example, Thomas Putnam questions Mercy, who is his servant, when he hears about the night's events.

Evaluation

- How did using role-play help you to explore the character's motivation?

- What did you learn about the questions raised in the play using this type of narration?

Development work on the play text

Act 1 explores the consequences of the girls' activities: the hysteria grows and the chain of events is set in motion.

Try it!

- Read Act 1 from 'How is Ruth sick?' to 'I say shut it, Mary Warren!'
- How does the role play activity on the previous page improve your understanding of the power struggles in this section?
- Explore this extract focusing on how you can convey power and fear. Consider the use of **space** and **levels**, **eye contact**, **silence** and **pause**. How can the silent girls communicate their reaction?
- Look closely at Abigail's speech beginning 'Now look you. All of you. We danced.' How can space, **movement** and **voice** be used to convey Abigail's power over the girls?
- Present your work

Evaluation

- What did you learn about the use of space, movement and eye contact in communicating the meaning of this section?
- Discuss your responses with members of your class. How do they feel about the characters? Where does your sympathy lie now?

Exploring contrasts and climax

The rhythm of a play has moments of intensity contrasted with moments of calm or tension. In *The Crucible*, there are scenes of great emotional power that are played in a tense, quiet mood. The opening of Act 2 with Elizabeth and John Proctor is a good example. These scenes contrast with climactic sections that capture the hysteria of the story.

In Act 3, the trial is taking place for witchcraft, in court. Mary is the servant of Elizabeth and John Proctor and they are now embroiled in the accusations. John has convinced Mary to reveal that all of the demonic fits have been pretend, and in what follows it is revealed that John and Abigail had an affair. Abigail denies it so John says his wife Elizabeth will confirm it. Elizabeth Proctor is brought before the court to answer Deputy-Governor Danforth's questions. The audience knows that her husband has confessed to adultery but Elizabeth does not. This creates tension: the questioning is measured, Elizabeth's answers are hushed as she tries to save her husband by denying the adultery, not realising that she is doing the opposite. The **climax** builds suddenly when Abigail pretends that she can see a bird (apparently 'possessed' by Mary) attacking her in the courtroom.

Try it!

- Read Act 3, set in the court room, from where Danforth says to Elizabeth 'Come here woman' through to 'GIRLS: (*raising their fists*) Stop it !!!'

- Discuss the tension created by the dramatic irony that the audience knows that Proctor has confessed to adultery but Elizabeth does not.

- In groups explore how the use of voice, pause, eye contact, proxemics and gesture can create tension, in the section up to 'ELIZABETH: (*faintly*) No sir'.

- Now consider how the pace changes and the climax builds.

- **Mark the moment** when Abigail pretends to see a bird attacking her in the court room and lets out her chilling cry. It is important to draw attention to her and to change the mood.

Abigail and Mercy need to make their imagined sight of the so-called 'yellow bird' seem real, so their voices might sound frightened – panicky. Danforth, as the senior figure of authority, may speak solemnly. Proctor could be mocking – he clearly does not believe Abigail sees anything.

- Explore the way the girls copy Abigail's tone and movements. The climax is built through the exact mirroring of Abigail's voice and action: every aspect must be the same, especially the direction of their gaze.

Evaluation

- Discuss how different groups showed the tension and hysteria in the scene. How did they use voice, pause, eye contact and gesture?

- What were the effects on those watching?

- How effective was the use of marking the moment?

The girls and John Proctor in the courtroom

Using forum theatre to examine John Proctor's moral anguish

Act 4 of *The Crucible* is tense and ultimately tragic. Proctor has to decide whether to confess and save his life or go to the gallows. His pregnant wife, Elizabeth, is brought to his cell to persuade him to save himself. The passion and intensity of the scene between Proctor and Elizabeth is powerfully moving but in order to play it with conviction you need to understand Proctor's moral choice.

Examine these lines:

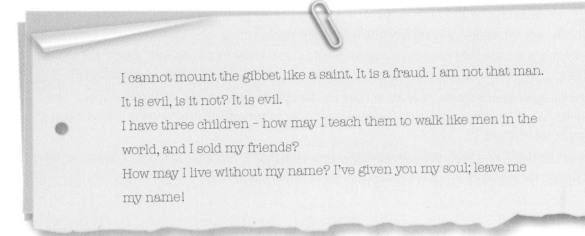

I cannot mount the gibbet like a saint. It is a fraud. I am not that man.
It is evil, is it not? It is evil.
I have three children – how may I teach them to walk like men in the world, and I sold my friends?
How may I live without my name? I've given you my soul; leave me my name!

What do these lines tell you about Proctor's moral dilemma? Feedback ideas by selecting explorative strategies, elements of drama and/or the drama medium and using them to communicate what Proctor means by these lines.

Try it!

Forum theatre enables you to explore the options faced by a character. In this scene Proctor wants to save his life but ultimately cannot betray those who died by telling a lie.

- One person becomes Proctor and the other Elizabeth.
- You can either use the text or improvise the scene in the jail.
- The remainder of the group divide into two sides, each representing one of the characters.
- At any point in the scene, they can stop the action and advise their character what to say next. Alternatively, someone can take over the role.

Evaluation

- How did this activity help you to understand Proctor's stark choices?
- Did any key lines or phrases make an impact on you?
- What would you have done in Proctor's situation?
- When and why did members of the group intervene? What did they suggest and how did this develop the arguments?

Designing a play set in a historical period

When a designer approaches a text for which he/she wants to recreate a specific period of history in a realistic way, the first task is to research the period visually. This will involve finding accurate information about buildings and the materials used to construct them, furniture, fabrics and colours used in clothing. Puritan America is a very well documented period and the characters and events in *The Crucible* are real.

Try it!

- Draw a diagram showing the use of space in *one* of the scenes you worked on.

- Indicate how any elements of set and props were included.

- How could you have suggested the historical period in the scene by adding light, sound and simple set (e.g. chairs or stools) and props (e.g. a bible)? What colours and materials would you use?

- A set designer must consider how the set can be changed to suggest four different locations. The creative use of key pieces can alter the appearance of the set without involving too much time and effort in set changes.

- The set for this play is likely to be very minimal to fit with the Puritan ethic in the play. However, for set design for almost all plays, remember that less is often more!

A set design for a production of The Crucible. Notice how minimal it is.

Example from a documentary response

Here is what one student wrote in their documentary response about the use of lighting as a symbol of what happens.

In our cauldron scene, we removed one of the green stage lights and placed it inside our 'cauldron' so it shone upwards. This helped us to set the mood of the scene, because the green light illuminated the faces of the actors and made them appear mysterious and sinister. We chose green light specifically for a number of reasons. Firstly in English folklore the colour green was symbolic of witchcraft and devilry, which we thought was appropriate. Secondly, green traditionally represents envy, which we thought mirrored Abigail's envy of Goody Proctor when her husband chose to stay with her. Finally, green is associated with sickness and nausea which we thought represented the 'sickness' that the girls suffer from during the play.

We used contrast to draw the audience's attention to specific parts of the stage and to make our scenes more appealing to the eye. In this scene we contrasted the green light in the cauldron with warm, yellow lights. This was meant to show the audience that the contents of the cauldron were evil and unnatural. Moreover, this contrast between the cool green light and the warm yellow light made the audience focus on the centre of the space where most of the action took place. This was our way of keeping the audience interested and engaged in the scene because we were showing them where to look and how to react to what they saw.

edexcel examiner comment

This shows aspects of both levels 1 and 2. The first paragraph demonstrates outstanding justification of the use of the medium and lighting. The candidate shows outstanding perception of the use of symbol to focus attention. The response could have been improved by exploring the use of other mediums and elements in conjunction with lighting.

Documentary response to the practical exploration

The documentary response is your final record of the six-hour exploration that you will complete under controlled conditions. It can contain photographs, sketches and diagrams with annotation, but no more than 1000 words in total.

Assessment

Your documentary response will be assessed on your analysis and evaluation of your and others' work and your understanding and appreciation of the way the medium and elements of drama are used to interpret a play.

Below are some short extracts taken from students' documentary responses. How far does each of them show what they did, how they did it and how effectively they used the mediums and elements of drama?

> The main scene we explored is at the climax of the play, and represents the moment when the truth comes out.

> I was given the role of the main character, and had to answer questions in the courtroom, using the strategy of 'hot-seating'. It was as if my character was on trial, and it helped me realise the pressures he was under and his motivation.

> Our group looked at how we might use lighting to bring out the contrasts between the main villain and the heroic protagonist, and we linked this to our ideas on the use of levels, so that while one character looked down from the raised area, she was lit up in this green spotlight and the audience could see she was in control...

> We brought out the contrast between the main characters using the lighting; it was important for the audience to know that each time a heroic figure entered he or she would be lit in a different way.

Making informal notes

It is likely that you will have been making informal notes on your practical work throughout Unit 2. You will have noted what explorative strategies, elements and mediums you used and how you felt these were effective in communicating meaning in your drama. These notes can be used later, when you are creating your formal documentary response.

There are many ways of recording your notes, for example, bullet points, spider diagrams, key words, sketches, grids, etc. The table below shows one option.

The strategies I/we used	Drama medium & elements	How it helped me to understand the play
First, our group used hot-seating… Then, I took on the role of… Finally, we marked the moment…	We showed the contrast between different characters by… The pace of the speech in this activity gave the impression that…	The contrasts were effective in emphasising the theme of… By taking on the role I was able to understand why…

Writing up your final documentary response under controlled conditions

When you write your formal documentary response, it will be in school under the supervision of your teacher.

In your final response to your practical work, try to show as clearly as possible how your drama was effective. As well as sections of writing, you can use drawings, sketches, plans, bulleted lists, grids or diagrams. You can choose the format which will make your response easy to understand.

Before you start your full documentary response, plan the overall structure of your work. You might want to divide the material into sections. Here is an example of just one possible plan, broadly in three sections.

Section 1: A brief overview of what play you and your group explored and what ideas, themes and issues you explored within it.

Section 2 : Show you how you and your group used strategies, elements and mediums to explore the action, characters, ideas, themes and issues of the play. Show how the section(s) you have explored connect to the play as a whole.

Section 3: Conclusion – draw things together and reflect on your work and what you have learned. Remember to evaluate the effectiveness of your own and also others' work.

Response to live performance

You will have the opportunity to observe a live performance as a member of the audience. This might be a professional production or a play performed by other students at your school.

Afterwards you will write an evaluation of the performance including your thoughts on the way in which the play was directed, acted and designed. This evaluation should be a maximum of 2000 words.

You will write up your final evaluation in school under the supervision of your teacher. You may use any rough notes you have made on the performance to help you write your evaluation.

Assessment

In your final response to a live performance you should aim to make critical judgements which are well justified. You should explain why you feel a certain way about the performance. The quality of your writing is assessed, so you also need to make sure that your work is clear and well structured with correct punctuation, grammar, spelling and appropriate use of technical language.

On the day of the performance

On the day of the performance you will want to write notes to ensure you remember details of the production. However, you should avoid writing extensive notes during the performance itself as this can be distracting for other members of the audience. It will be a good idea to make a few notes in the interval.

One way of recording your observations is on a chart like the one below. This can also be a useful prompt to take into the performance with you to make sure you have covered all the key points.

What you have observed	What effect this had
General • What is the title of play and who is the playwright? • What is the venue of the performance? • What is the theatre company or the performers, if not a professional company? • What is the date of the performance?	How do the factors of choice of play, venue, timing and performers affect your expectations of the performance? Is the play in a particular genre which leads you to expect specific drama mediums and elements?
Performance area/staging Just *before* the play begins jot down notes on the *stage* and *performance* area: • What sort of stage is it (if there is a stage)? • Where is the audience positioned? • How did actors use the performance space? • How did the actors use different levels? • Did the performance space used suit the production?	How does this create an effect between the actors and audience? (Is it intimate? Distant? Like a circus ring? Find your own way of describing it.)

The performance – design elements What *lighting* was used? Think about: • light and dark, use of spotlights, etc. • colours. What *sound* was used? • Live? Recorded? • Music? Singing? Orchestra? Was any use made of *multimedia*, such as projections? What was the *set* like? • Did the set fit with the overall style of the performance? • Was there an overall 'look' or feel (for example, a dominant colour or idea, such as a tree that remains in view the whole time)? • To what extent was it 'realistic'? Was it set in a particular historical period? • Did the set change during the performance (for example, in each act)? How many locations were there and why? What were the *costumes* like? • Did the costumes fit with the overall style of the performance? • Was there an overall theme or look (for example, from a historical period, or everyone wearing masks)? • What did individual characters wear? Did any characters change costumes during the play? Note particularly the costumes of the main chaacters and the reasons for these.	Did these choices create a particular atmosphere? If so, what? What effect did this have on how we viewed particular characters?
The performance – acting and directing • Who were the key characters and what were they like? Were there any obvious stereotypes – e.g. villain/hero/clown? • What did the main characters do and what was their part in the action and plot? • What were the characters' main relationships in the performance? • What did you notice about how they used voice, movement and gesture? When did they use them? • How did the pace of the play change over time? Were there any particular scenes where the rhythm pace or tempo were especially noticeable? • Were there any particular moments of tension, climax or anti-climax? How were these created by the acting?	If so, why? How did it affect this audience's interpretations of the play? What effect did this have on the mood and meaning of the play at key points?
Overall response • What was your own overall impression to the play as a whole once it finished and why? • What was the audience's reaction (both during and at the end of the play)? • What did other members of your class or group feel about the play and why?	

Remember to fill out as much as you can of the right-hand column, thinking about how the points you observe affect your understanding of the play as a member of the audience. You will want to add to these notes later on, after the performance itself.

Below is an extract from one student's notes after they went to see a play.

My notes

Acting

- Main character very quick movements … and loud, aggressive voice effectively showing the tension and his anger at this point in the play.

- Scene 2 use of space effective with girlfriend when they argue … They stood very close together which effectively communicated their feeling of claustrophobia.

Design

- Lighting v dark and threatening during storm. Use of special fx – thunder. Created suspense and atmosphere of foreboding when characters came on stage …

After the performance

- Expand your notes on the different things you observed in the performance and what effects these had. Add any further details and fill in any gaps.

- Check factual information: get the names of characters and plot details right (especially if it is a play you have not studied before). Use the programme, if there is one.

- Make sure you get your 'on the spot' impressions down: you need to make sure you remember the effect of the production on the audience and on you at the time, while it is fresh in your mind.

Check your notes against the different areas of the Programme of Study listed in the first section of this book.

- Have you thought about all the **elements of drama**? Which ones were used particularly effectively within the play you saw?

- Have you covered use of the **drama medium** within the play?

Think about what effect the use of these elements and mediums had on your understanding of the play. Remember that the elements and mediums will often be linked. For example, the medium of sound can help create tension and the element of climax, and movement, mime and gesture are a key aspect of characterisation.

Structuring your response

Once your notes are complete, you may wish to group them into key areas.
You could sequence your notes, too, adding paragraph or section numbers
alongside the notes you have made. The structure below is an example.

Section 1:

- You could give the facts about the play: title, playwright, theatre company (if applicable), director, venue and style of theatre.

- You might want to outline your expectations of the play, based on any advance leaflets or advertisements, the genre of the play, the playwright and venue.

You could, for example, write sentences starting as follows:
The play/performance I saw was…
Before I saw it, I expected…
The performance took place in/on…
This had the effect of…
It also meant that…

Section 2:

- You could now discuss the performance area, the staging and set, the various locations shown and the effect that these things had on the interpretation of the play.

- Cover the lighting, the use of music, costume and props and how these linked to the plot and action, characterisation and other elements.

You could, for example, write sentences starting as follows:
The overall look/design of the production was…
This created the effect of…
The use of lighting/set/projection/sound was particularly effective at this point because…

Section 3:

- At this point you could discuss the action of the play, any key points of tension or climax, the rhythm pace and tempo of the play and its overall form.

- You'll also want to cover the key characters, the use of voice, movement, gesture and mime within characterisation and the type of language used.

You could, for example, write sentences starting as follows:
The key characters were…
The tension was built up at this point of the play by…
Use of movement was particularly effective here in order to…

Section 4:

- You could detail your overall response to the play and highlight any parts which you felt were particularly effective. What did other people feel about the play?

- Did the play fit with your expectations at the start?

You could, for example, write sentences starting as follows:
Overall, I judged the performance to be… because…
The character of… was particularly impressive because…
The use of… helped to convey…

Writing your final response to live performance under controlled conditions

The evaluation of live performance is a written account of the live performance you have seen (professional or amateur). It can be up to 2000 words long and should contain your evaluation of the effect and effectiveness of the approaches taken by the director, actors, designer, etc. The final piece will be written under controlled conditions but you can take in your notes to help you.

To get a mark at the higher levels it is important you do the following:

● Make clear, coherent critical judgements about what you have seen and at what point in the performance (don't make vague comments about the performance or give a few details).

For example:

> *The actress playing the Mother made two clear gestures in the final scene to convey her horror at what had happened. First, she clasped both hands to her face, as if to cover her eyes from what she had seen.*

●Write about the effect of decisions made by the actors, director, designer, etc. (for example, whether the set design conveys a particular idea and whether it works).

For example:

> *By using dark, crimson cloth for the background to the set, the effect was as if the whole play was taking part inside a beating heart which matched the passionate, revenge theme of the play.*

● Support what you say with evidence (it is no good saying 'the design didn't work' unless you describe the design carefully, what its effect was – and *why* it didn't work).

For example:

> *I was unconvinced by the way Ariel moved. He/she is supposed to be light and airy – that's what the script says, and so I expected him to have light, quick movements, but he moved slowly and heavily which wasn't right.*

● Pay attention to the quality of your writing in terms of spelling, punctuation and grammar (it is no good having great ideas if no one can understand them because of your poor sentence structure and use of full stops, for example), and use an appropriate style. Don't be over-chatty in your language – make it formal without being impersonal, like the examples above.

Try it!

Evaluating the evaluations!

This is a description of a response to live performance which would achieve a high level.

The evaluation of a live performance is outstanding. There are coherent, critical judgements that are informed and extremely well justified. There is an outstanding application of written communication. Spelling, punctuation and grammar are faultless and the selected form and style are appropriate.

Below you will find a number of extracts from responses by students. With this description of a high level response in mind, think about the following:

- Do you agree with the comments made by the examiners underneath each response?

- Can you see why they have made these comments?

- Where there are comments that indicate the answer could be improved, can you think how you would have improved what was said? Look at the four bullet points on the previous page to help you.

Student A:

> One actor who particularly impressed me was Reece. I was impressed with Reece because he played three different roles in the play just like the other 3 boys but I think that Reece done particularly well. He can change his voice and put himself into a completely different character. For example when he played the girl he changed his tone of voice and when he walked on stage he was strutting. Also he had different hand gestures and movements such as he puts his hand on his hip and flicks his head as if he has long hair to flick over his shoulder. However when he was a bouncer he had more of a fierce, serious, threatening face and a stronger, manly time of voice.

edexcel :::: examiner comment
Gave opinions, and seemed to understand the narrative (plot) but rather descriptive, tending to tell what happened without saying much about the effect.

Student B:

> Music is incredibly important to the play as it is a musical. It is used to build up tension and to emphasize emotion. I am focusing on the background music rather then the songs. The music was brilliantly directed and used with such expertise that I made the piece seem dreamlike and otherwordly at time, while at others bringing the action so close to you that you felt as if you were a part of it yourself. They used it at times, such as Mrs Lyons' descent into madness or Mickey's rage, to create shock and at others to calm the piece and create bonds with character's.

edexcel :::: examiner comment
Focus on music as a drama element is very good – an intense response is conveyed through a fluent style/language, but examples need more development (how was it used?) to get a higher level.

Try it!

Student C:

B was extremely successful in his performance of Macbeth; this was because all the way through the play his internal and emotional struggle was evident through his monologues and reactions to the other actors. However, because of the theatre's outdoor setting sometimes his monologues were hard to be heard. What was most successful about B's performance I think was his movement. Rather than using large, exaggerated gesture and using the space of the stage by pacing and moving about, B chose to fix his character in certain positions and to only respond subtlety to his fellow characters and although his movement was limited, every motion and gesture had an intensity about it and it was his subtlety in acting that really brought out what Macbeth was going through emotionally at the time.

edexcel examiner comment

A personal response with good evaluation; fluent and lucid with ideas very well supported. Understanding of the play, the characters, the medium and elements all very clear too.

Student D:

The two blocks, which were placed on the floor beneath the wire which were close together and easily accessible via the wire, could signify two choices for the characters. They were used to symbolise good and bad, for example, at the first scene of the play, when Sam was addressing Sagar, they communicated contrasting vibes and were placed on oppostie sides of the stage. so it seemed that they were opposites in their choices. The lighting on these blocks created a shadow that is part of the name of the play, suggesting several things:

- Every choice has a risk, a possible bad consequence
- When making choices, good or bad, your previous intentions if they were different will always be attached to you somehow.

This contrast was shown by the way the actors used voice, body and movement. Sam was bellowing his words as if attacking Sagar. He was obviously distressed about something and was letting his anger out on her. His voice was angry and aggressive because of how loud and fierce it was. Sagar's voice was timid and afraid compared to Sam's. She only spoke when spoken to which reflected her fear and anxiety. Her posture showed signs of distress, because she was hunched forwards and constantly looking down. She fidgeted constantly with her camera, repeating the same little hand movements that showed her anxiety. Sam was doing exactly the opposite. He was constantly moving across the stage almost like he was looking for answere or something to blame.

edexcel examiner comment

This response shows a coherent, clear analysis of how staging is used within the performance. The positioning of the blocks is neatly linked to a practical example of how the actors worked on the stage and there is a high level of personal response in place as well assured understanding of the themes of the play, linked to the staging. The student then goes on to link the ideas about contrast and choices to vivid examples of how the actors used the medium of drama in terms of voice and movement, making analytical comment about what was communicated to the audience. There is a real sense of understanding evident in terms of the characters' emotions and relationship.

The student then goes on to link the ideas about contrast and choices to vivid examples of how the actors used the medium of drama in terms of voice and movement, making analytical comment about what was communicated to the audience. There is a real sense of understanding evident in terms of the characters' emotions and relationship.

Unit 3: Drama Performance

What will you do in Unit 3?

In this unit you will work as part of a group to create a performance. This will be shown to an examiner who will mark you as an individual.

The theme each year is set by the exam board, for example 'Freedom', but there are a number of choices for your group. You can present:

- a **devised** piece based on a stimulus or a devised performance of a Theatre in Education piece
- a performance of a **scripted** play, which could be a complete short published play, an extract from a longer one or a selection of scenes
- a mix of devised and scripted material.

> **Key terms**
> - devised drama
> - scripted drama

How are you assessed in Unit 3?

Unit 3 is worth **40%** of your total GCSE marks. You can choose to be examined as a performer or as a designer who provides a design skill for the production. Whichever option you choose, each of the four areas of assessment below are worth **10%** of your marks.

Performers will be marked on:

- vocal and movement skills
- roles and characterisation
- communication with other performers and the audience
- understanding of the production's content, style and form.

Designers will be marked on:

- response to the needs of the planned ideas
- reasons for design decisions in the context of the production
- the design skill demonstrated during the performance
- how the design enhances the performance.

Performance times must be no less than 15 minutes for small groups and no longer than a maximum of 45 minutes for a group of nine.

How will this book help you with Unit 3?

This section gives advice about creating and developing characters, planning rehearsals, vocal and movement skills and advice on each of the performance support options. Throughout the section there are 'Try it!' boxes, some with examples of how other students have used the suggestion. You can try out these ideas in your own work.

The Performance Process

The process of creating any performance is called rehearsal, but there are many preparatory stages you need to undertake before you can begin working on a full, polished piece of drama. Rehearsal can take many different forms but will always lead up to a live production. You should approach each of your drama lessons as a rehearsal.

The purpose of a rehearsal

Each rehearsal must have a clear aim that sums up what your group wants to achieve. Early rehearsals will focus on exploring the theme, character and script while later sessions will aim to polish scenes. It is a good idea to set the aim for the next lesson at the end of each rehearsal. Always be specific. For example, notice the difference between the aims to the right, set by two different groups for a rehearsal of *Blood Brothers*.

> **Aim 1** To improve the scene where Mickey and Eddie first meet

The first statement shows that the group has realised that the scene is not working very well but they have not identified why or what they need to do about it. In the second statement, the group has obviously discussed the problem and identified that the scene is not working because it is not very funny. They have gone a step further in analysing what makes the scene funny and concluded that it is the significant differences in the characters.

> **Aim 2** To develop the differences in the characters of Mickey and Eddie to increase the comedy in their first meeting

There is a detailed example of a well-planned rehearsal on page 177.

The performance and the space

You need to be aware of your performance space from the very start of the performance process. Think about how you want to relate to your audience. You might want to consider the points below.

- Will you be on the same level as your audience or higher up?
- How much space do you have available? Will you use it all?
- What are the sightlines of your performance area? Will the entire audience be able to see you everywhere?
- How many entrance points to your performance area will there be for the actors?
- Are there any special technical effects or specific scenery that you intend to use which will restrict the space?

Try it!

Working in your group, discuss and plan how you will use the performance space in your drama.

How to use rehearsal techniques

In the past, a director would tell the actor where to stand and how to move and how to say their lines. This is usually referred to as 'blocking' and is rarely used nowadays. The contemporary director Katie Mitchell jokingly calls this 'park and bark' directing.

Most modern directors work with actors to explore the text and find reasons for movement and vocal tone. This makes their performances much more truthful because the performers have experienced the characters' emotions and reasons for action. You should explore and experiment in your rehearsals as a group.

Leading up to the exam

In the final weeks before the examination you will be making the final preparations for your production. You might choose to have two key rehearsals at the end of the process. These are suggested below, but depending on your piece of drama and the resources you have available this preparation period may vary.

The technical rehearsal

This session concentrates on the elements of performance support: other students who may be examined in this area or non-examinees may be involved.

- Go through the production from **cue** to cue: this means that every time there is a sound effect, costume change, lighting effect or set change you play this section and make sure that the technical element is correct.
- During this rehearsal the acting is not important but you should try to perform at the correct speed so that cues can be timed accurately.

Technical rehearsals are very important and time should be allocated to make sure that everything is right.

Key term
• **cue**

The dress rehearsal

You may not have extensive costumes, but the purpose of the 'dress' rehearsal is that it is as close to the real performance as possible. It is a good idea to invite a few friends to make the occasion seem like the exam. You should treat this as if you were being assessed. No stopping! If there is a problem you must try to overcome it without losing focus and concentration.

Your teacher and others in your group will give feedback to both the actors and members of performance support. Make sure that you spend time resolving problems as soon as possible, as there is little time left before the exam.

edexcel examiner tip
Ensure your performance meets the time limits set for Unit 3. Make sure you check the timing of your piece when there is still time to shorten or lengthen it if necessary before the exam.

Organising a scripted performance

154

A scripted performance is an exciting journey, taking the work of a playwright from page to stage through exploratory work, and making it your own. Every production of a scripted production is unique because of the idea and interpretation brought to it by those involved.

Any scripted play you work on will need to be linked to a theme set by the exam board for that year. For example, if the theme is 'Loss', one of the plays below might be suitable.

Play	How the play fits with the theme
My Mother Said I Never Should by Charlotte Keatley	Loss of childhood innocence
Whose Life is it Anyway? by Brian Clark	Loss of physical movement
To Encourage the Others by David Yallop	Loss of life
Our Country's Good by Timberlake Wertenbaker	Loss of freedom

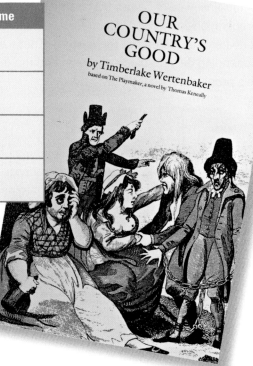

OUR COUNTRY'S GOOD
by Timberlake Wertenbaker
based on The Playmaker, a novel by Thomas Keneally

Choice of play

You need to choose the play that will help show the strengths of the individuals in your group and allow you all to have the opportunity of meeting the marking criteria for the exam. It will depend on:

◉ how many people are in your group

◉ what style of play you prefer

◉ what you enjoyed studying or seeing in the theatre during your course

◉ particular skills the members of your group can use in their work.

Casting your play

Remember that you will not always have the same number of actors as parts in the play, and that you can cast some or even all actors in **multiple roles**.

It might also be the case that you need or want to use **cross-gender casting**. If you are playing a role of a different gender, consider what effect this will have on the whole piece. Some plays lend themselves to it more easily than others. For example, you may find it difficult to play a sensitive love scene with an actor of the same gender, but some roles – for example, 'Doctor 1' in Olwen Wymark's *Find Me* – can be played equally well by a male or a female actor.

The genre of your play might affect the casting. Non-naturalistic plays often involve stylised scenes where actors play inanimate objects. In Mark Wheeller's *Hard to Swallow* there is a scene where the cast become kitchen objects. If your play is more naturalistic, you need to consider how well suited each actor is to the part and how well they will be able to show their acting ability.

Key terms
• multiple roles
• cross-gender casting

155

Try it!

Working in your group, discuss your choice of play and how you will cast the roles. Decide whether you will:

- use cross-gender casting
- cast actors in multiple roles.

Think about the genre of your play and how this might affect your casting choices.

Rehearsal techniques

The importance of planning rehearsals was discussed on page 152. Here we will look at some techniques that you can use to explore the play and to make the journey from 'page to stage'.

Sections and titles

Divide the play into sections and give each one a title. This helps to tell the story of the play and enables you to focus on what is happening in each specific part. For example, you might title the section in *The Tempest* where Prospero insults Caliban, 'Prospero's Cruelty'. When you are planning rehearsals you can focus on one section at a time and not feel that you should get through a set number of scenes or a whole act.

Building tension and suspense

Go through the play and note the key times when you want to build up the atmosphere or tension. Then decide what effect you want to achieve and what skills you will use to create the desired impact. Your examiner will be awarding marks for the effect you have on the audience.

In *The Crucible* by Arthur Miller there is a scene where Abigail Williams accuses another girl, Mary Warren, of witchcraft. Abigail and her friends pretend that Mary has sent out her spirit in the form of a yellow bird. The tension here could be created through vocal tone, eye contact and movement.

Try it!

Working in your group:

- divide the play into sections and give each one a title
- note the scenes where you want to build the atmosphere or tension. Discuss the effects you want to create and mediums of drama you could use to achieve these.

Abigail and the other girls pretend to see Mary's spirit in the form of a yellow bird

Focusing on relationships

Your rehearsals will need to examine the key relationships in the play. You can explore your characters' attitudes and feelings through **hot-seating**, through improvising events that are suggested but not scripted or through examining the text for clues. You can then consider how the skills of voice and movement can be used to convey the emotions in performance.

Try it!

In *Blue Remembered Hills*, the character Donald Duck is abused by his mother, bullied by other boys and teased by the girls.

Read this example of how a student approached the role of Donald and then make a list of rehearsal techniques that you could use for your own character.

- Improvise a scene where his mother hits him, focusing on *why* rather than how.

- Hot-seat the other characters to discover why they bully and tease Donald.

- Write down all the things that other characters say about Donald to build a picture of how he is seen by others.

- Consider how the information gathered will inform the use of voice and movement.

- Identify three key moments in the play where Donald gains sympathy from the audience.

The character of Donald Duck in a production of Blue Remembered Hills

Organising a devised performance

Devising theatre is an exciting and rewarding experience. You will be experienced in the techniques used in Unit 1 for exploration of stimulus and these skills will be important when creating your original piece of drama. Many professional theatre companies devise their work and playwrights often workshop their ideas with actors before writing the script.

When deciding on your material, think about the skills and interests of your group.

- Consider work that you have enjoyed in Units 1 and 2.
- Bear in mind plays that you have seen at the theatre.
- Ask yourselves: 'What are we trying to say?' This helps to clarify the meaning of the piece.

Working in a group

A useful strategy for successful group work is to know each person's strengths and personality and allocate responsibilities accordingly.

Some groups like to set up an agreement or contract about how they will work together on their Unit 3 project. Look at the example below.

DRAMA PERFORMANCE CONTRACT

We will always attend our drama lessons unless we are unwell.

We will phone or text someone if we are not going to be in the lesson.

We will complete research or other tasks by the agreed deadline.

We will leave all important notes at school so that they are available in every lesson.

We will give everyone in the group a chance to put forward their ideas.

Responding to the theme and your stimuli

The exam board will set a theme each year. The stimuli which you will use as starting points for your drama are likely to be chosen by your teacher and will link to this theme in some way.

However, if you are choosing your own stimuli, one of your first steps in gathering your initial ideas might be to create a mind map. Look at the mind map below, which is a group response to the theme 'Conflict'.

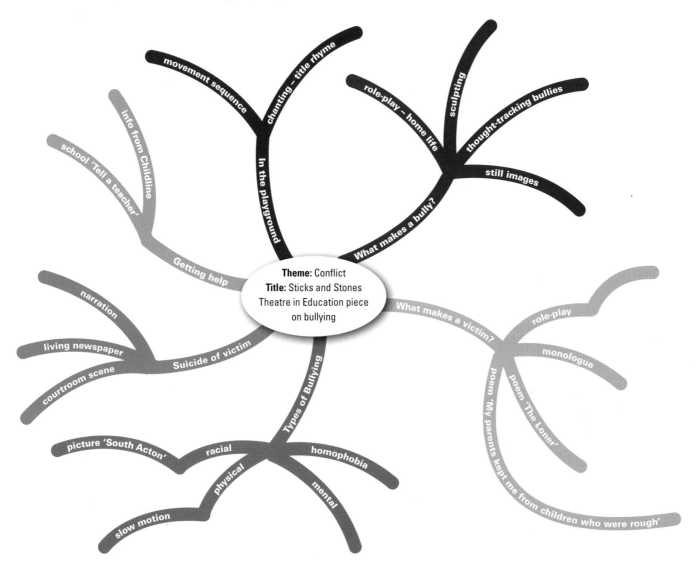

Try it!

Using the theme 'Freedom', create a mind map with your group.

- Include general topics, then become more specific, suggesting stimulus material.
- Note any ideas for the use of drama techniques that come to mind at this point.

160

Try it!

What makes a good response to the given theme?

Look at the statements below and decide whether or not you agree with them. If your group response is negative to three or more of the statements, you might want to modify your idea or try out an alternative one from your mind map.

Our idea is original.

We are all excited about this approach.

We can use many different drama techniques.

We have found material that we can use.

We will all be able to contribute to the creative process.

Each member of our group will be able to demonstrate his/her abilities.

We have something to say to our audience.

Planning your time

Make sure that you do not spend too much time creating your piece, leaving insufficient time to polish it for the examination. One way of avoiding this is to draw up a timetable, working back from the exam date. For each week, aim to know what you are going to do ('Activity'), who is going to do what ('Who will do it') and what you are hoping to achieve ('Aim').

Try it!

This is an example of part of a rehearsal plan. Create a similar plan for your own work.

	Activity	Who will do it	Aim
Week 1	Research topic	Student A – Internet Student B – newspapers Student C – library Student D – interviews	To gather materials and ideas
Week 8	Technical and dress rehearsals	Whole group Performance support from Year 10 to assist	To polish to exam standard

Shaping the drama

The devising process should begin with research: this might involve reading, finding poems, articles or stories, interviewing people or watching documentaries or films.

edexcel examiner tip

Try to think about how research can lead to drama. Sometimes students have excellent research material but do not realise its dramatic potential. For example, do not overuse a narrator to convey facts, but perhaps introduce the information in a dialogue.

Put it in the bag!

Early in the process you will be experimenting with ideas and creating drama that is not polished. At this stage you should not reject work nor should you work for too long on one aspect. Keep a notebook or folder with all your plans, ideas, diagrams of movement sequences and examples of dialogue. This will ensure that you do not forget the details of sections that you have worked on.

The 'put it in the bag' technique means that you record your work and then move on to another exploration. After a number of lessons, perhaps every two weeks, you 'empty the bag' and review what you have done. Some ideas will be worth keeping and developing while others may be rejected.

Here is an example from a piece of drama on transportation, on the theme of 'Loss' (of liberty), inspired by a theatre visit to *Our Country's Good*.

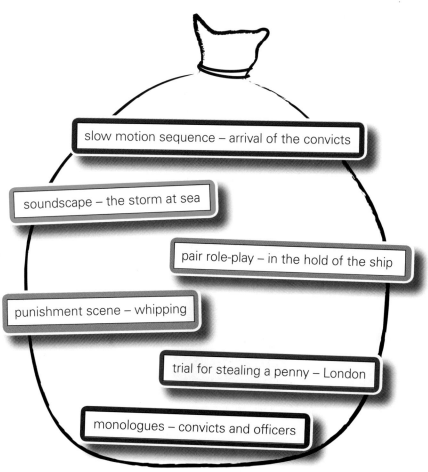

slow motion sequence – arrival of the convicts

soundscape – the storm at sea

pair role-play – in the hold of the ship

punishment scene – whipping

trial for stealing a penny – London

monologues – convicts and officers

Try it!

In your group, look at your weekly plan and decide when you will 'empty the bag' one last time and move to the final stages of rehearsal.

Remember, if you keep on devising new sections until the final week, your piece will lack finish and may even be too long. See page 153 for advice on technical and dress rehearsals.

Organising a mixed performance

The opportunity to create work that combines a published play with other published works and original material can be thought-provoking and inspiring. You will be using your knowledge and understanding from Units 1 and 2 in creating this original work.

You could:

- create a performance based on a scripted play using sections of the text mixed with original material. For example, you could improvise scenes indicated but not shown in the script and a new ending.
- devise a piece based on the assignment brief that includes sections from a play mixed with poetry, song lyrics, fiction and factual material.

What are the advantages of this approach?

- You can use the skills of all members of the group, which might not be possible in a scripted performance.
- You can include a wide range of material.
- You have a clear starting point to work from, but can also be creative and original.

Note that it is important to ensure that your piece has a clear meaning and intention rather than being a jumble of interesting ideas.

An example of a mixed performance

Below is an outline of how one group approached the assignment brief 'Loss', using the play *Whose Life is it Anyway?* by Brian Clark as their base text. Their work combined the scripted text with new scenes, movement, masks and original music.

About the play

Ken Harrison, a sculptor, suffers a serious spinal injury in a road accident. After six months of intensive treatment in hospital, doctors tell him that he will never walk again or regain the use of his arms. Ken's brain is functioning perfectly but he will be dependent on full-time caring for the rest of his life. The action of the play traces Ken's fight to be allowed to die with dignity. The play is thought-provoking but at times very amusing.

A production of Whose Life is it Anyway? where cross-gender casting has been used and Kim Cattrall plays the role of Ken

Outline of students' planned performance

Broken Statues

Scene 1: (devised) The doctors discuss how to tell Ken that he will never walk again.

Scene 2: (scripted) Dr Emerson tells Ken the truth about his future.

Scene 3: (devised) Movement sequence accompanied by original music showing the accident.

Scene 4: (devised and scripted) Scene where the occupational therapist visits Ken cross-cut with sequences showing Ken working in his studio. Students become the life-size statues.

Scene 5: (scripted) Comic scene where an orderly jokes with Ken.

Scene 6: (scripted) Ken instructs a barrister to act for him.

Scene 7: (devised) Dream sequence – movement, original music overlaid with Dr Emerson's words. The sculpted statues become lifelike and advance on Ken, echoing Dr Emerson's words.

Scene 8: (reworking script) A collage of lines from the text, giving opinions about what Ken should do, interspersed with the judge's final decision.

This piece of drama gave students opportunities to work in a variety of mediums. Those with skills in movement choreographed sequences, others improvised new scenes and some worked from the original text. Most students were involved in all aspects of the piece.

Performers
Voice

A vast range of emotions, intentions and desires can be conveyed through a character's voice. The voice can also indicate status, nationality and age.

How can you use your voice effectively?

It is important that the audience can hear and understand what you are saying.

- Breathe correctly to avoid losing volume at the end of a speech.
- Project your voice to the furthest point of the performance space. Even when you are whispering, you must be heard.
- **Articulate** clearly, even if you are speaking with an **accent**.

You will be assessed on your use of **pace**, **pause**, **pitch** and **tone**.

- Pace is the speed at which you speak. Pace indicates age, creates mood or atmosphere and can add tension.
- Pause refers to short breaks and stops in your speech to create effects. You can use pauses to show uncertainty, indicate thought or heighten mood.
- Pitch is the high or low level of the voice.
- Tone is the quality of the sound of your voice. The tone and pitch of your voice show how the character feels as well as defining age or status.

As well as words, other vocal sounds can communicate to the audience. Consider the effect of a yawn (boredom), a sigh (regret), a gasp (shock) or a laugh (amusement).

> ### Key terms
> - articulate
> - accent

Try it!

Read this short section from Louise Page's play *Tissue*.

M:	Bags I be doctor.
W:	I'm the nurse.
M:	You're the patient.
S:	Why?
M:	Because I'm the doctor and she's the nurse so you've got to be.

- Play this dialogue at a fast pace to show that the children are young and excited about their game.
- How might the pitch and tone vary to indicate the status of each speaker?

Movement

At its most obvious, movement is how you get from one place to another, but gesture, stillness, eye contact and pace combine to create credible characters who an audience can believe in.

Age, mood, emotion and status are shown through movement. A mannerism, such as twisting a lock of hair when nervous, can add important detail to a role. Subtle gestures communicate emotion, a touch sometimes says more than words. Eye contact shows feelings and can draw attention to unspoken thoughts.

The pace and fluency of movements and the impact made by entrances and exits should reflect the genre of the play. A fast-paced comedy will require quick movement whereas melodrama requires an exaggerated style. Physical theatre is **symbolic** but movement that is more natural can also have symbolic meaning.

The mind map below traces the many aspects of movement. You can continue to add branches, going into more and more specific detail.

> **Key term**
> • symbolic

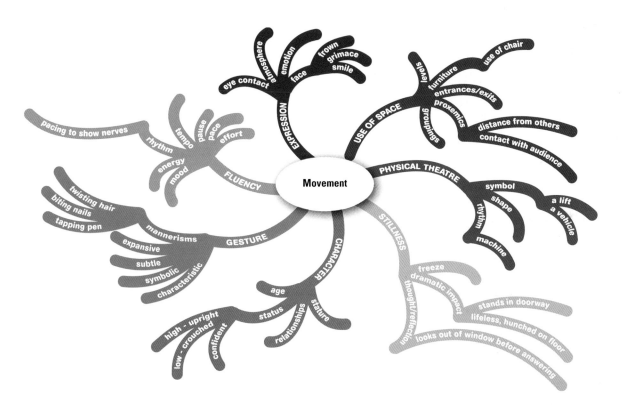

Imagine you are playing Juliet in Shakespeare's play *Romeo and Juliet*. In the balcony scene you could use movement in many different ways:

- twirling hair in a flirtatious gesture
- sudden movements into the room to reassure the Nurse
- lingering eye contact with Romeo
- a mocking glance at the 'inconstant moon'
- symbolic clasping of hands
- stretching, indicating the effort of peering over the balcony
- stillness watching Romeo leave.

> **Try it!**
>
> In your group, discuss the different ways you could use movement in your own performance.

Voice and movement in rehearsal

In your rehearsals work on using your voice and movement to convey *emotions* (how I feel), *objectives* (what I want) and *intentions* (why I say this). When you are preparing your role think about why you say the lines and to whom you are speaking. Consider the *effect* you want to have on the other character or audience. Remember that emotions inform movement.

Think about the way the actors in the example below might use voice and movement.

FATHER: I am your father and I forbid you to leave this house!

Vocally you might decide to speak this line as a low, menacing whisper, rather than to shout it. You could move slowly towards her in an intimidating way.

I *feel* angry and frustrated

I *want* my daughter to stay at home

The *intention* is to *reprimand* her

DAUGHTER: I can see that you are angry but I wish you could understand my reasons.

Here, your voice could be soft and gentle with an unvoiced pause before touching his arm as you say 'I wish…'

I *feel* upset that he is angry with me

I *want* him to reconsider

The *intention* is to pacify him

How voice and movement can convey feelings and intentions

The scene at the top of the facing page is from *The Crucible* by Arthur Miller, which is set in 1692. Here, Elizabeth is suspicious because her husband, John, has had an affair with a younger woman. John is trying to rebuild their relationship but resents her cold mistrust.

Discuss the scene and explore how these feelings and intentions can be conveyed in various ways. Below are some examples.

Elizabeth: Sharp tone in first sentence, unflinching eye contact, stillness, pause – an unspoken accusation. Then she turns away, and speaks more harshly with an accusing tone for the second sentence.

John: Strides purposefully towards her, stress on the word 'planting', upward **inflection** on 'forest edge' – emphasising how much work he has done. Then he puts out a hand to touch her, stops, shrugs, sits down slowly at the table.

Key term
• inflection

Try it!

Here is another scene from *The Crucible*. A group of girls have been dancing and trying to contact spirits in the woods, encouraged by Abigail. Their religion forbids such activities. Below are possible ideas on voice and movement for the character of Abigail in this short extract.

MARY: What'll we do? The village is out! I just come from the farm; the whole country's talkin' witchcraft! They'll be callin' us witches, Abby!

MERCY: She means to tell, I know it.

MARY: Abby we've got to tell, Witchery's a hangin' error, a hangin' like they done in Boston two year ago! We must tell the truth, Abby! You'll only be whipped for dancin', and the other things!

ABIGAIL: Oh, we'll be whipped.

MARY: I never done none of it Abby. I only looked!

MERCY: Oh, you're a great one for looking aren't you Mary Warren? What a grand peeping courage you have.

VOICE: Stress 'whipped' with a sarcastic tone. Use a low, menacing pitch.

MOVEMENT: Move quickly across to Mary, grab her shoulder aggressively, turning to face me

I want Mary to take equal responsibility

My intention is to intimidate Mary

Imagine that you are playing Mary or Mercy. Write notes to show your objectives (wants), intentions (effect on others) and emotions and indicate how you will convey these with your voice and movements.

Roles and characterisation

Characterisation is the process an actor undertakes to capture the nature, personality and attitude of the person he or she is playing. In devised work, you will be creating your own roles and characters; in scripted pieces, you will interpret a character created by the playwright.

Try it!

Think about the role you are playing. Ask yourself the following questions. If you are performing a scripted play, look for the answers in the text.

- How do I see myself?
- What do other characters think about me?
- What do I say about other people?

Describing your character in a script

Here is an example of a student describing his role of Macbeth.

Macbeth

I say about myself:	'Let not light see my black and deep desires'
	'I have no spur to prick the sides of my intent, but only vaulting ambition'
	'O full of scorpions is my mind'
	'I have almost forgot the taste of fear'
Others say about me:	'For brave Macbeth, well he deserves that name'
	'He is full so valiant'
	'I shame to wear a heart so white'
	'this dead butcher'
I say about others:	(of Banquo) 'kind gentleman'
	(of Duncan) 'has been so clear in his great office, that his virtues will plead like angels'
	(to Lady Macbeth) 'Bring forth men-children only'

My analysis of Macbeth's character is that he begins the play as a brave and well-liked soldier but he allows himself to be influenced by his wife's ambition. Macbeth had respect for Duncan and a close friendship with Banquo but became paranoid after the first murder. His fear caused him to continue the killing and by the banquet scene he had become insane.

Patrick Stewart playing the lead role in Macbeth at the Gielgud Theatre

Describing your character in a devised piece

You need to think through your character's background, the life they led before as well as the recent events which led up to the situation portrayed in your devised work. We can call this information the backstory.

Key term
• backstory

Try it!

Draw a diagram like the one below and include all the important facts about your role.

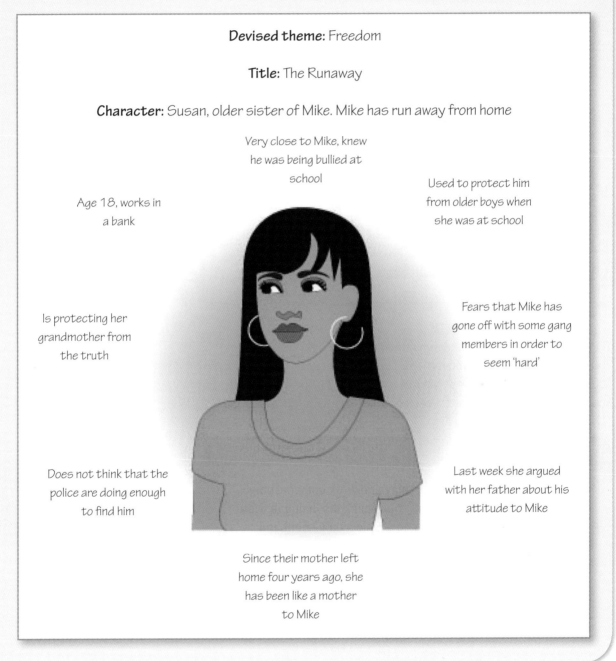

Devised theme: Freedom

Title: The Runaway

Character: Susan, older sister of Mike. Mike has run away from home

Very close to Mike, knew he was being bullied at school

Age 18, works in a bank

Used to protect him from older boys when she was at school

Is protecting her grandmother from the truth

Fears that Mike has gone off with some gang members in order to seem 'hard'

Does not think that the police are doing enough to find him

Last week she argued with her father about his attitude to Mike

Since their mother left home four years ago, she has been like a mother to Mike

Other ways of exploring your character

● Create a 'role on the wall' showing how you feel inside and how others see you (see page 88).

● **Hot-seat** each character in your piece to discover their emotions and backstory.

170

What does my character want?

Whenever we speak to someone in everyday life we are driven by what we want. This can be the need to comfort, to be comforted, to find out information, to give information, to attract attention, to be friendly, to be critical, and so on.

In Mark Wheeller's play *Hard to Swallow* we can examine the 'wants' of two characters, Simon (Catherine's brother) and Maureen (Catherine's mother). Catherine is an anorexic teenager whose family struggle to cope with her illness. In this scene Maureen has argued with Catherine for refusing to eat her meal.

SIMON:	(*Entering*) What's happened now, Mum?
MAUREEN:	It's all my fault.
SIMON:	It's not Mum. She's got to learn.
MAUREEN:	There are ways and means … but what I've just done is not the right way for Catherine … I don't know what else I can do … I've tried everything. Oh Simon … I just couldn't see it through.

I want to support you

I want you to reassure me that it isn't my fault

I want you to know that I am on your side

I want you to help me because I am at the end of my tether and feeling very guilty

This exercise helps you to see why the characters say certain things and it enables you to add movement, gesture and vocal tone to communicate your emotions. Maureen could put her head in her hands and speak through controlled weeping when she says 'It's all my fault'.

Try it!

Take a scene or section of your play and work out what your character's intentions are when they speak the dialogue. Note how to communicate this in terms of voice, movement and gesture. Refer back to pages 52–53 to remind yourself about these points.

171

Your character's journey

Every character in a piece of drama makes a journey. This journey can be both physical and emotional. Your character might begin and end in the same room or town but make a significant emotional journey.

It is helpful to map out your character's journey, noting the physical and emotional changes as the play progresses. The map below traces the story of Derek Bentley, which one group of students used to explore the theme of 'Injustice'.

Background

Bentley was sentenced to death on 11 December 1952 for killing a policeman during a break-in at a warehouse in Croydon, Surrey. The court was told his co-defendant, Christopher Craig, fired the fatal shot but because he was still a juvenile in the eyes of the law he escaped the death sentence.

THEME: INJUSTICE

Derek Bentley's Journey

Family protect him. Frustrated. → Makes friends with Chris Craig. Family disapprove. Confused. → Night of murder. Chris calls for Derek. Happy to be part of Chris's world.

In jail. Confused. Wants to go home. ← On the roof. Terrified at police sirens. Arrested and shouts 'let him have it' (gun). ← At warehouse Derek does not understand what is happening. Thinks it is a game. Afraid and anxious.

The trial distresses him. Has an epileptic fit in the dock. Petrified. → Execution day. Derek does not understand what will happen. Play ends as he is led out.

Try it!

Chart the journey of your character, as in the example above. Consider key moments in the plot and indicate both what happens to the character and how he or she feels. This will help you to develop your performance.

Mood boards

You could make a mood board for your character, using text and images from magazines and newspapers to summarise a character's personality and appearance. The images can be abstract, for example, barbed wire might represent a character who is defensive and sharp.

Communication

Communication is an important aspect of your production. The aim of any performance, whether it is scripted or devised, is to share the ideas with those watching and to communicate your intentions clearly.

The visiting examiner will be in your audience. He or she will be able to judge how effectively you communicate with other members of the ensemble and with the audience. Your research, character development and focused rehearsal will enable you to communicate the meaning of the piece.

How do I communicate?

There are many techniques that an actor will use during a performance to communicate with the audience and other cast members.

- **Eye contact:** Think about when and why you have eye contact with another character or with the audience. There are times when you will communicate your emotions or intentions by making strong eye contact.

   At other moments you might *avoid* eye contact, for example to conceal guilt. In *The Crucible* there is a famous scene in the courtroom where Elizabeth Proctor is being interrogated. She avoids looking at the judge because she is about to tell a lie.

   Sometimes the actor will make eye contact with the audience. This generally happens when you are acting as a narrator. When doing this, try to make eye contact with several different audience members rather than looking over their heads or addressing just one person.

Try it!

What does this picture communicate to you? How does the use of eye contact add to the meaning of this moment?

Choose two moments from your drama: one where a character makes eye contact and one where he or she avoids looking at someone. What is the difference? What does this communicate to the audience?

- **Gesture:** The use of gesture communicates the fine details of your character to an audience and can also draw reactions from another character, for example, pointing angrily in an argument or touching an arm gently to comfort someone.

- **Pause:** We have looked at the use of pause in the section on Voice and movement. Pause is very useful in communicating emotions or creating dramatic tension. A pause before a humorous line adds to the impact in comedy – a stand-up comedian often puts in a slight pause before the punch-line.

Scene from a production of Mary Goes First *at the Orange Tree Theatre in Richmond*

Try it!

Consider your script or devised dialogue and identify some key moments when a pause would help to communicate something to the audience: perhaps a comic scene or a moment when some shocking fact is revealed.

- **Narration/monologue:** These techniques enable an actor to speak directly to the audience. A **narration** communicates the story and a monologue reveals the character's emotions and intentions. Puck in *A Midsummer Night's Dream* tells the audience what he is planning to do to the lovers in the forest. He is speaking directly to the audience, who are drawn into his plan.

- **Rapport:** It is very important to have a good relationship with the whole ensemble. During the performance, there will be times when you are not the centre of the action and you may not have any lines. It is vital that you continue to focus on the action, react as appropriate and show that you are fully involved in the piece. At other times you may have to move items of set or props. Make sure that you do this with energy and efficiency and stay in role throughout the performance.

Content, style and form

What do these terms mean and what will you be examined on?

Content

What the drama is about

You will be examined on:

- your understanding and appreciation of the material

- your awareness of the meanings created in the drama.

Style

The genre of the piece (see below). Style can sometimes be associated with a significant dramatist, e.g. a 'Brechtian' style means it is closely associated with the work of Bertolt Brecht.

You will be examined on:

- the methods and techniques that you have used to create your performance.

Form

The shape and appearance of your production.

You will be examined on:

- the effectiveness of the drama strategies you employ

- the structure and selection of appropriate techniques.

When creating your production you can refer to the **elements of drama** (see pages 46–55) and the **explorative strategies** (see pages 10–25).

What is genre?

Genre is the *type* of drama: it is used as a way of putting plays and performances into categories which have the same features. 'Thriller' is a genre in which you would expect a story full of suspense, perhaps a murder or a ghost, and a succession of tense, frightening moments. *The Woman in Black* is an example of this genre.

Try it!

Here are some genres. Name one play for each genre, but if you get stuck, check their definitions in a dictionary.

| Comedy | Tragedy | Musical | Historical drama |

| Melodrama | Epic | Verbatim |

Here is an example of planning notes for a devised piece of drama, summarizing content, style and form.

Theme: Freedom
Title: Sold into Slavery

Content: *From slavery to freedom*

- Freedom in Africa
- Capture and the slave ship
- Life on the plantation
- Protest and the fight for freedom
- Free at last

Form: *Stylised with some realistic scenes*

- Chorus: scenes linked by a chorus of slaves who comment on the events
- Monologues: slaves tell the audience their story
- Dance/movement: freedom in Africa and the capture of the slaves
- Natural dialogue: on slave ship/plantation/ protest meetings

Style: *Dramatisation of historical events*

- Montage: short scenes like a collage in sections. Each one tells an aspect of the story
- Greek tragedy: a chorus of slaves links scenes

Try it!

Use a large sheet of paper and create a map of your ideas for your exam piece.

- For devised work, you will decide how to use style and form to communicate the content.
- If you are working from a script, you should examine what the writer wants to communicate, explore the style of the play and identify how you will shape your own unique interpretation of the text.

edexcel examiner tip

You will be marked on how well you control the chosen style and form: examiners are looking at the effectiveness of your choices. You need to make sure that you have the desired impact on your audience. For example, with the piece above, the examiner would be assessing how successfully the monologues of the slaves communicated with the audience.

Shaping the production

Once you have decided on the theme, topic or play text for your performance exam you should plan your time carefully. You will draw on what you have learned from Units 1 and 2 to shape the final production.

If you are devising your performance, this stage might involve finding out about events, people and opinions as well as exploring ways in which professional companies create original drama. If you are working from a script, you might research the playwright's background, the context in which the play was written and any other information that will help you to create your role(s).

Try it!

Look at this example of a group's research which was undertaken for a performance of *Blue Remembered Hills*. The play is set in 1945 and is about a group of seven-year-olds on a single afternoon in the Forest of Dean. Note how the group expressed their research points as questions.

Now make a list of your own research points relevant to your drama work for Unit 3.

- Where is the Forest of Dean?

- What can we find out about the way the characters speak? What do the slang words mean?

- What was life like for children in this part of the world during WW2?

- How did rationing affect the way that they dressed?

- What toys did children play with at this time?

Rehearsal

This is the journey from the ideas (devised) or the playwright's words (scripted) to the finished performance. Your work during this period should be tightly planned and have very clear intentions. Rehearsal could be described as a 'focused experiment': this means that your work will have a clear aim but should allow for exploration of ideas.

Here is an example of a well-planned rehearsal.

Aim: *Scene 3 – To develop our characters to make them more believable.*

Rehearsal methods

- Hot-seat each character to discover their backstory and feelings.

- Improvise events that are revealed during the hot-seating.

- Identify important moments where the background informs the content.

- Explore how voice and movement can be used to convey character and emotion.

- Play the scene, focusing on conveying emotions and intentions.

- Discuss how the rehearsal work improved the scene and set aims for the next rehearsal.

edexcel examiner tip
You should always be aware of how you will be marked. Notice how this group have included voice and movement in their rehearsal plan. This shows that they have considered how their experiment can be linked to the exam assessment.

Try it!

Plan a rehearsal with your group.
- What do you want to achieve by the end of the session? Set a specific aim.
- Now decide how you will use drama techniques to reach your goal. Do not try to include too much.
- Consider the length of your rehearsal. Remember that it is more effective to have a definite purpose than to simply 'go through the scene again', which is an approach that will only reinforce any weaknesses rather than improve the performance.

Performance Support

The creation of a piece of theatre involves many technical experts as well as performers and directors. When you visit the theatre you will be aware of the set design, the lighting, the sound and music and the costumes. In Units 1 and 2 you will have explored how these elements can enhance the practical exploration of the stimulus or text.

For the Unit 3 exam you may select one of the following options, rather than performing:

- lighting
- sound
- setting and props
- costume
- masks or make-up.

What does this option involve?

- Working with the group in deciding how your designs will reflect the meaning and enhance the performance
- Researching and experimenting with design ideas
- Keeping notes throughout the process
- Finalising your design, discussing it with the group, then creating the finished product
- Organising the equipment and operating it (or supervising the operation) on the day of the exam
- Creating a portfolio that documents the whole process
- Making a five-minute presentation to the examiner

edexcel ::: examiner tip

A maximum of *three* performance support students may work with a group. Only *one* student in each performance group may offer any one option. For example:

- one lighting designer
- one sound designer
- one costume designer.

You can only offer *one* option for one performance. This means that you would not be allowed to offer set design *and* lighting, for example.

Try it!

In this production of *Macbeth*, notice how the lighting creates shadows and silhouettes. What does the costume tell you? Can you work out which scene in the play is shown?

Lighting design

Students choosing to be examined as lighting designers have usually had an opportunity to learn about lighting during the course. Many have explored the use of lighting during Units 1 and 2 while others might have been involved in performance support in extra-curricular drama productions. It would not be wise to choose lighting for Unit 3 unless you have had some prior experience.

What is required for Unit 3?

You will:

◉ work with your group to discuss the needs of the play

◉ research the play/topic as well as lighting equipment

◉ check the equipment at your centre and hire any additional lanterns

◉ create a design with a grid plan and lantern schedule

◉ create a lighting plot or cue sheet with at least four lighting states

◉ make a presentation to the examiner.

What is the purpose of lighting?

Lighting can communicate:

◉ location

◉ weather

◉ time of day or night

◉ mood

◉ atmosphere

◉ a focus on a specific point or character.

Here are some lighting notes a student made after a visit to Headlong Theatre's production of *Faustus,* a play about a man who sells his soul to the Devil:

Try it!

Read the example below, then think about the last time you went to the theatre. Write down five lighting effects that communicated information to you.

Look back at pages 32–33 for a reminder on successful stage lighting

• The hard-edged spotlight made me focus on the candle.

• The atmosphere was eerie as the sharp circle of light was very bright but the surrounding stage was dark.

• The lighting designer had subtly lit the actors' faces and upper body.

A Headlong Theatre production of Faustus, with lighting by Malcolm Rippeth

The lighting design process

Discuss the play or topic with your group. Remember that you are part of the creative team and not simply responding to a given list of instructions.

Make some notes about how you think that lighting might communicate important details and add to mood or atmosphere. At this stage, you should not be concerned with how you will achieve the effects.

Research the theme and background to the play/theme. Your research could include looking for photographs of lighting from professional productions.

Do an audit of the facilities and equipment at your centre. How many lanterns do you have? How many dimmers are available on your lighting board? Do you have a supply of gels, frames and gobos? Will you need to buy anything? Do you have a budget?

Sketch your visual ideas and then match this with the equipment audit.

Use a **ground plan** of the set or performance space and work out how many lanterns you will need to create the effect. Draw up a **lantern schedule** indicating exactly how you will use each lantern.

Make a list of cues and effects in your script. A cue sheet shows exactly when a lighting change happens and over how long. Remember that you must have at least four different lighting states.

Arrange for the lighting to be rigged, according to your **grid plan**. Try out the effects. **Rigging** involves hanging the lanterns and patching them into the dimmer board.

Create a detailed plan of your lantern schedule and rigging.

Key terms
- **ground plan**
- **lantern schedule**
- **grid plan**
- **rigging**

edexcel ▓ examiner tip
Try to avoid blackouts. These can make the performance disjointed and break the audience's concentration. It is much better to cross-fade from one lighting state to another if you want to suggest the passage of time or a change of location.

Sound

Digital technology gives a sound designer a huge range of possibilities in recording, manipulating and playing back effects. Sound provides an added dimension to the performance: it can place a location with a single stroke, it can alter the mood or it can shape an emotional response.

What is required for Unit 3?

You will:

◉ create at least four sound effects – one of them must be created and recorded live

◉ record the sound onto a CD/mini-disk

◉ create a cue sheet detailing the order, length and volume of each sound

◉ operate the sound, or supervise its operation, in the exam performance.

To do this, you might want to:

◉ work with your group to analyse the opportunities for sound

◉ research sound effects and check the equipment at your centre.

Look back at pages 30–31 for a remiunder on successful use of set and props

Acoustic and recorded sound

Sound can be divided into two categories: **acoustic** sound, which is produced live, and **recorded** sound.

Sound communicates essential information to the audience. Some sound effects are vital to the plot or meaning, for example, the car driving away at the end of *Death of a Salesman*. Other sound effects are **ambient**: they are used to create atmosphere, for example, distant thunder adding to the tension in a thriller.

Key terms
• acoustic sound
• recorded sound
• ambient sound

Try it!

Using a grid similar to the one below, suggest a sound effect that would communicate the following information to the audience. The first row has been completed for you.

Information	What is communicated?	How?
Dramatic impact	Tragic ending	Slow drum roll
Time of day		
Weather		
Place		
Atmosphere		
Emotional response		

The sound design process

Discuss the use of sound with others in your group.

Research the play/devised topic and look into where sound effects can be found or created.

Make sure you have a good knowledge of what is required, and what is possible in the centre.

Check the equipment available for creating, recording and playing sound effects.

Obtain, create and compile effects and music.

Transfer these as necessary onto appropriate formats for playback.

Prepare sound plans and equipment plans: this documentation outlines all sound requirements and includes a cue sheet showing order, length and output level of each cue.

Develop and refine your plans according to the production requirements.

Work closely with other aspects of performance support so that all elements work together to enhance the production.

During the performance, work from your cue sheets to operate or supervise the sound.

Make a presentation to the examiner, outlining your research and decisions.

edexcel examiner tip

- Remember that sound often synchronises with other technical effects. For example, if your performance involves a thunderstorm, you will need to synchronise sound and lighting.

- Remember that the examiner is awarding marks for the effectiveness of your sound design in performance as well as the accompanying documentation.

Set and props

The set designer creates the world in which a play takes place. This involves understanding the theme, period, time of day and location, then discussing the interpretation. The set designer will need to do some research, then sketch and make a detailed model of how the set and props will work in the performance space.

Look carefully at the photo opposite, which shows the set for *Dealer's Choice*, a play by Patrick Marber.

- What does this set design communicate about the location?
- What do you notice about the colour and texture?
- How do the props and the set work together to convey the atmosphere and place?

What is required for Unit 3?

You will:

- work with your group to establish the needs of the piece
- make sure that there are opportunities for a set/prop designer to meet the exam requirements
- research the play/topic
- measure the performance space accurately/list the props needed
- sketch designs leading to your final decision
- locate materials for constructing the set/props; find any necessary furniture/props
- create a scale model of the final design as it appears in the performance space
- make a scale ground plan and/or scale drawing of any designed props
- work with performers to ensure that the set/props can be used easily in performance
- make a presentation to the examiner.

> **edexcel examiner tip**
> Set and prop design can be time-consuming. Make a detailed plan that allows you time to prepare sufficiently. The aspects of the set should be ready well in advance of final rehearsals. If you are still painting the set the day before the exam, the performers will be very frustrated!

You might want to keep a log of your preparation work to jog your memory later on in the course, for example, when you come to make your presentation. Look back at pages 36–37 for a reminder on successful use of set and props.

The performance space

Make an early decision about the space where the play will be set. Remember that the actor/audience relationship will be affected by the choice of performance space.

The meaning and the practicalities

The set and props convey the message of the play so your designs must echo the intentions of the group. Examine the practical needs of the piece such as the entrances, doors, number of locations and specific references to furniture or props.

Colour, texture, shape and proportion

Set and prop design convey a message visually to the audience. The designer should consider the desired impact of the set as well as its practicality.

184

Here are some notes prepared by a student set designer.

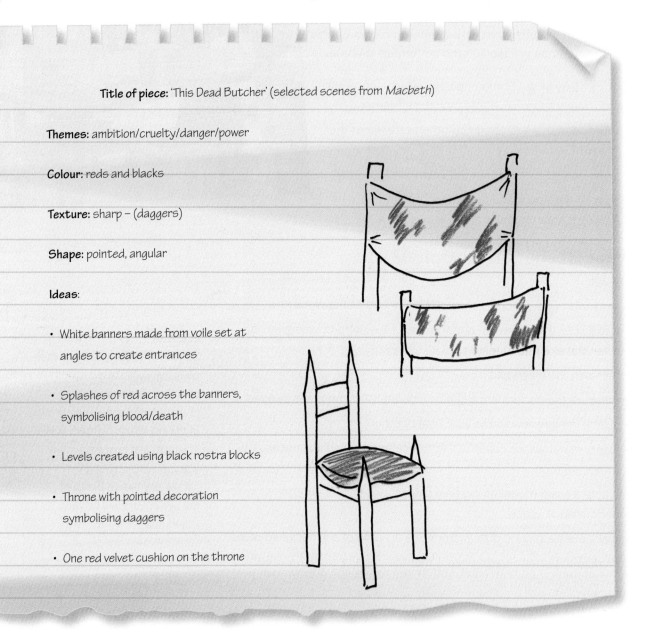

Title of piece: 'This Dead Butcher' (selected scenes from *Macbeth*)

Themes: ambition/cruelty/danger/power

Colour: reds and blacks

Texture: sharp – (daggers)

Shape: pointed, angular

Ideas:

- White banners made from voile set at angles to create entrances

- Splashes of red across the banners, symbolising blood/death

- Levels created using black rostra blocks

- Throne with pointed decoration symbolising daggers

- One red velvet cushion on the throne

Try it!

Make notes similar to those above for your exam piece.

edexcel ▓ examiner tip

- You will need to ensure that your ideas are practical in an exam environment. If another group is being examined directly after you, any set or props will need to be changed quickly and easily.

- Stay aware of health and safety issues for yourself and others when creating and using props. This is particularly important when there are quick set and prop changes involved.

Costume

Costume conveys information about the characters, adds to the mood and atmosphere of the production and can communicate time, location, weather or period.

The costume designer is responsible for planning the **costume plot**. This will involve discussing the intended meaning of the play with your group, researching the play and its period, sketching initial designs, selecting fabric and materials and measuring the actors before making the costumes.

Key term
• **costume plot**

In theatre, the costume designer has assistants who make the costumes and help actors to make changes during performances.

What is required for Unit 3?

You will:

◉ discuss the costume design with your performance group

◉ research the play/topic, then make sketches of costume ideas

◉ measure the performers accurately

◉ create the final design for at least two costumes

◉ either make or find at least two costumes

◉ create the costume plot or list of costumes/accessories worn by each actor

◉ oversee the costumes in the performance

◉ keep a detailed log of all your preparation work

◉ make a presentation to the examiner.

Look back at pages 26–27 for a reminder on successful use of costume.

Realistic or symbolic costume?

If your play is set in a particular period, you will need to research the clothes worn at that time. This will include finding out about materials, textures and shapes. As costume designer, you will take this information and interpret it for your production.

When you are making your costume, you should consider the status of the character. A rich or royal person might wear velvet, silk or brocade whereas a poor character would wear less expensive fabrics. To make a costume look worn or shabby you can rub it with sandpaper or a cheese grater.

Symbolic costumes can be used when actors are playing multiple roles. An actor could add a hat or shawl to indicate a change of character. The items need to be chosen carefully to communicate quickly and effectively. They should also be easy to change in and out of swiftly. As a costume designer, you will need to consider the most effective way to communicate the character using minimal costume changes. Sometimes symbolic costume can suggest abstract characters such as Death.

Try it!

Look carefully at the costume worn by this actress, Frances Barber, playing Cleopatra in a production of Shakespeare's *Anthony and Cleaopatra*.

- What does the fabric tell you about the character's status?
- Note the decoration on this costume: comment on the designer's decisions.
- What does this colour suggest to you?
- What is the significance of the headdress?

Important details

- Remember to ensure that the costumes do not restrict the actors' movements on stage.
- Discuss your ideas with the lighting and set designers to ensure that the colours and fabrics do not clash.
- Accessories are important to the finish of your costumes. Think carefully about hats, shoes, jewellery, etc.

Making and hiring costumes

Costumes can be made from recycled garments or inexpensive materials. Charity shops and jumble sales are great sources for clothes and fabrics. Costume hire can be expensive, so check prices and your budget carefully before ordering.

What is a costume plot?

This is a list or chart showing which characters appear in each scene/section, what they are wearing and any changes throughout the play. It enables you to keep track of where a costume needs to be for a quick change and it details the costume needs of every character.

> **edexcel ▦ examiner tip**
>
> - Remember that if performers need to change costume, you will need to make sure your costume is easy to get in and out of quickly.
> - Think about where you position the costume, in relationship to where the performer will come off and re-enter the performance space.
> - Fit the costume well in advance so that any alterations can be made and the performer has a comfortable, well-fitting costume.

Try it!

Complete a costume plot chart similar to the one below for your production. You can add more scenes and sections if necessary. The first section has been completed with an example from a production of *Blood Brothers*.

Character	Scene 1	Scene 2	Scene 3	Scene 4
Linda	short dress sandals plaits in ribbons	black skirt school tie white shirt blazer black shoes	jeans sweatshirt trainers	tracksuit bottoms baggy cardigan slippers

Masks and make-up

The make-up artist or mask designer creates 'faces' for characters in the production. Make-up and masks can be realistic, fantastic or symbolic. Modern lighting has reduced the need for heavy make-up and the modern actor will use very little when playing naturalistic roles.

Make-up and masks are very important for stylised, fantastic or symbolic productions, for example, the Inca masks in *The Royal Hunt of the Sun* or the make-up for the fairy characters in *A Midsummer Night's Dream*.

The procession scene from a production of The Royal Hunt of the Sun at the National Theatre

What is required for Unit 3?

You will:

- discuss the needs of the play or devised piece with your group
- research the period, characters and materials
- sketch design ideas
- measure actors for masks or photograph faces for make-up
- check for allergies to make-up products
- create the final design for at least two masks and/or make-ups
- create designs for all other masks and/or make-up used by the actors
- fit masks and/or practise applying make-up
- apply make-up and/or oversee the use of masks for the exam performance
- keep a detailed log of your preparation work
- make a presentation to the examiner.

Look back at pages 28 and 29 for a reminder on successful use of masks and make-up

Reflecting conventions and concepts

Make-up, like masks, reflects character and genre, so it is important that your designs tie in with the conventions of the performance. Your first task will be to understand the overall concept of the production, to find out if it is naturalistic, stylised, symbolic or fantastic.

Research for a play set in an historical period will involve finding out about how people appeared during that period, including whether they wore make-up and how fashion affected their appearance. For example, *Playhouse Creatures* by April de Angelis is set during the Restoration in the seventeenth century.

Make-up

Make-up includes the creation of scars and blemishes. If you are designing this type of make-up, you will need to research techniques and materials.

Fantastic and non-human characters offer creative opportunities for the make-up designer. For example, a devised piece based on *Dracula* or a children's theatre production of *Alice in Wonderland* would afford excellent opportunities for make-up design.

edexcel examiner tip

Remember that if taking the make-up option, you need to consider how far the chosen performance provides opportunity to demonstrate your skills. If the performance is naturalistic the make-up will need to be subtle and not over-done; other performances may require special effects.

Try it!

Look carefully at the photo, which is from a production of *Macbeth* set in modern Africa.

This make-up for one of the witches recreates a 'witch doctor'.

- What is the effect of this make-up?
- What does the make-up suggest about the character?

Masks

Mask theatre originated in ancient Greece and has been part of the theatrical tradition ever since. Masks have a powerful effect in theatre.

There are several forms of mask:

- Full mask – covers the whole face, e.g. the chorus in *Women of Troy*
- Half mask – leaves the mouth uncovered, e.g. *The Servant of Two Masters* commedia characters
- Eye mask – covers only the eyes, e.g. *Romeo and Juliet* at the masked ball
- Full head mask – covers the whole head, e.g. *The Insect Play* insect characters
- On-head mask – the face is visible, e.g. *Equus* wire masks for stylised horses

edexcel examiner tip

When creating a mask, make sure that an audience can clearly hear the performer through the mask, and that the performer can see properly.

Independent research

Find out about the Trestle theatre company, who specialise in masked theatre. You might also research Greek theatre and **commedia dell'arte**, where masks were very important. Can you use these ideas in your work?

Key term
- commedia dell'arte

Examzone examzone

As the date for the exam gets closer you will be finalising your preparations for the important day. The final two or three days before your performance are crucial. You should make sure that everything is in place in order to avoid last-minute panic.

- You may well want to have a final rehearsal a few days before the exam. You might need time to make adjustments (see pages 152–153).

- However, do not make significant changes to your work at the last minute.

- Do not rehearse for too long the day before – you want your piece to be sharp and fresh, not stale.

- Make sure you know what time your exam will take place and where you need to go.

- Get there early. You may need to set off earlier than usual.

- Make a list of any items you have promised to bring and put them out the night before.

- Have an early night. You need to be alert for the performance.

How to relax and control nerves

Breathing deeply always helps in coping with butterflies. Support the rest of your group, including performance support candidates, who will be nervous too. Avoid playing games – they simply tire you out and you need energy to focus and concentrate. Make sure that everything is ready. Nothing is more nerve-racking than having to run around finding a costume or prop at the last minute.

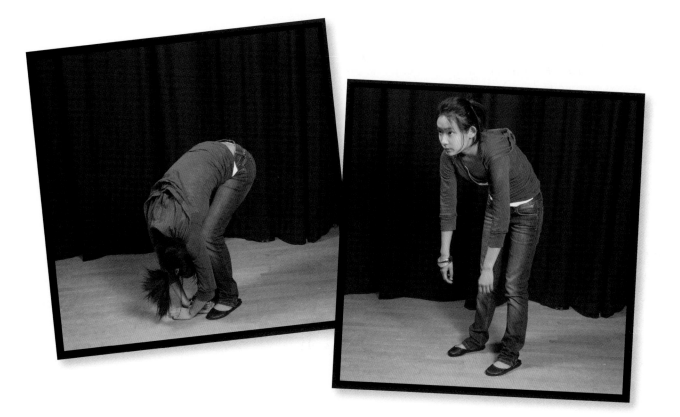

Checklists

Performers

- Do I know my lines and movements?
- Where are my props?
- Do I have all the items for my costume? What about shoes and accessories?
- Have I prepared some exercises that will help me to get into character?
- How will I warm up/relax before the exam?

Lighting/sound/set and props

- Have I checked that all lanterns, dimmers and sound equipment are working?
- Have I run through every lighting state and checked that furniture is correctly placed?
- Have I run through every sound cue and checked levels and volume?
- Do I have everything I need to create live sound?
- Do I have my cue sheet and script? Is there sufficient light for me to read it during the performance? If not, I need a small torch/lamp.
- Is the set correct in every detail?
- Have I checked sightlines?
- Is everything in a good state of repair?
- Are all the props positioned correctly for the actors to collect?
- Have I checked the set under stage lighting, making sure that everything is in the right place?
- Is my presentation complete and rehearsed?

Costume/make-up and masks

- Have all the costumes been fitted and altered as necessary?
- Are costumes positioned for quick changes? Do the actors need help?
- Do I have all the materials I need to complete the make-up?
- Have I allowed sufficient time to make up each actor?
- Have masks been fitted carefully? Can the actors speak and see?
- Do any masks need repair following use in rehearsal?
- Is my presentation complete and rehearsed?

Glossary

Term	Definition
accent	Characteristic pronunciation determined by the region, country or class of the speaker
acoustic sound	Acoustic sound is live. See also ambient sound and recorded sound.
ambient sound	Ambient sound creates atmosphere (e.g. birdsong). See also acoustic sound and recorded sound.
aesthetic	Relating to appearance. It can often be linked to beauty
articulate	To speak distinctly and accurately
back projection	Images or photographs shown on the cyclorama or a back wall of the performance space
backstory	The events that have happened before the action of the play
commedia dell'arte	A style of comic Italian drama involving masks and stock characters
costume plot	A plan indicating which costumes are worn by each performer in each part of the play and where costume changes occur
cross-gender casting	Males play female roles and/or females play male roles
cue	A signal – word or effect – that prompts action from an actor or technician
devised drama	A scene or play created through improvisation, sometimes involving research
dialogue	The spoken language in a performance or text between two or more people
dramatic irony	The audience know something important but the characters in the play are not aware
ellipsis	Shortened or unfinished sentences
empathy	Understanding of someone's feelings
evaluation	An assessment of the effectiveness or significance of the drama work
flashback	Playing events from the past
floodlight	Stage light covering wide area
gels	Material placed in front of a lantern to create coloured light
genre	A dramatic form that has identifiable characteristics. Some examples of genres are comedy, tragedy and thriller
gobo	A metal cut-out placed in front of a lantern to project an image
grid plan	A plan of the lighting grid indicating where each lantern is hung and which dimmers they are working on
ground plan	A 2D diagram of the performance space indicating the positions of set, furniture, entrances and exits
inflection	A variation in tone or pitch of the voice
juxtaposition	Placing close together in order to make a comparison

Term	Definition
lantern schedule	A plan of the actual lanterns (lights) used, the areas lit and the effects created
meta-theatre	A device used by playwrights where the actors in the play are performing a play – a play within a play
monologue	A lengthy speech performed by one actor revealing feelings or commenting on events
montage	Used by Brecht and in film. The putting together of short sections or scenes that are dissimilar
multiple roles	Performers play many different characters in the same play
naturalistic	Tending to show characters behaving in natural ways
physical theatre	Using the body to present inanimate objects in a stylised way
proxemics	The physical relationship between the performer and the audience or between the performers in the space
realistic	Like naturalism, attempting to show life as it 'really is'
recorded sound	Recorded sound is any effect created in advance. See also acoustic sound and ambient sound.
rigging	Putting up the lanterns on the lighting rig and focusing them onto the performance space
scripted drama	A play written by a playwright
slow motion	Choreographed movement to represent action performed slowly
soliloquy	Speech in which actor talks directly to audience as if revealing thoughts. This term is usually used if the actor is alone on stage or at least isolated from the other characters
soundscape	The creation of atmosphere with vocal and percussive sounds
spotlight	Stage light focused on one single place
stereotyping	A fixed or shallow idea about a person, place, etc.
stylised	Does not attempt to look 'real'
symbolic	Being representative or emblematic
total theatre	Productions that include many non-verbal aspects of the drama mediums such as masks, mime, dance, music, sound, chanting, puppets or lighting
unreliable narrator	A narrator whose words you may not be able to trust